ORIGAMI TOYS
That Tumble, Fly, and Spin

Paul Jackson

GIBBS SMITH
TO ENRICH AND INSPIRE HUMANKIND
Salt Lake City | Charleston | Santa Fe | Santa Barbara

To my son **JONATHAN**, age 5.
You taught me the joy of
sharing origami toys.

First Edition
14 13 12 11 10   5 4 3 2

Text and illustrations © 2010 Paul Jackson
Photographs © 2010 Avi Valdman
Hand model: Chen Ozeri

Published by
Gibbs Smith
P.O. Box 667
Layton, Utah 84041

1.800.835.4993 orders
www.gibbs-smith.com

Designed and produced by Dawn DeVries Sokol
Printed and bound in the China

Manufactured in Shenzhen, China in December 2009 by Toppan Printing Co. (SZ) Ltd.
Gibbs Smith books are printed on either recycled, 100% post-consumer waste, or FSC-certified papers or on paper produced from a 100% certified sustainable forest/controlled wood source.

Library of Congress Cataloging-in-Publication Data

Jackson, Paul, 1956-
  Origami toys : that tumble, fly, and spin / Paul Jackson. -- 1st ed.
      p. cm.
  ISBN-13: 978-1-4236-0524-9
  ISBN-10: 1-4236-0524-1
  1. Origami. 2. Paper toy making. I. Title.
  TT870.J322 2010
  736'.982--dc22
                          2009027530

CONTENTS

ACKNOWLEDGMENTS

A book that is more than thirty years in the making accumulates many people to whom I owe a debt of thanks. In origami, I particularly thank Bob Neale and Seiryo Takekawa for their inspiration; also John Smith, Dave Brill, Mick Guy, and the late Eric Kennaway, all of the British Origami Society, for their encouragement and wise words down the years, especially when I was much younger and certainly much sillier. My thanks also to the many origami societies, magazines, publishers, and authors around the world who have so generously given me forums in which to teach and publish my origami toys and other models—your support for my work has been invaluable. Finally, for her support during this project, my love and thanks to my wife, Miri Golan, the most extraordinary person in my life and in origami today.

INTRODUCTION

A successful origami toy is an appealing combination of good design and innocent delight. The very first model I designed was a toy (the Flapping Bird 1), and ever since then, my greatest satisfaction in origami has come from designing interactive toys that flap, jump, fly, spin, swim, bang, tumble, turn inside out, peck, snap, rock, and talk.

For me, a successful toy is the most satisfying form of creative origami. This is because to be considered a success, the mechanism must function well, and this functionality is the result of a design that is refined in both its concept and its folding sequence. With noninteractive models, the concept and the folding sequence are almost always compromised to achieve a degree of representation or "realism," but when a model is designed to move, these cannot be compromised or the mechanism will not function well.

The best origami toys, then, have an inherent directness and clarity—they seem somehow pure or obvious, to have been *discovered* in the paper, not contrived from it. However, behind this apparent obviousness often lies a great deal of work. Some of my toys were folded into endless variations before I decided that one variation—and only one—was somehow the best, the most perfect realization of an imperfect idea. These variations were always in search of an apparently effortless merging between a mechanism that operated to its optimum efficiency, the aesthetic appearance of the completed model, and a fluent, concise folding sequence. When I had the balance right, I would know it. The key word to describe my favorite pieces is *elegance*.

My origami toy heroes are Bob Neale (USA) and Seiryo Takekawa (Japan). Both these creators have designed origami toys of supreme originality and elegance. In today's origami world, where mathematical complexity and representational details rule, these simple, charming toys can easily be dismissed as naïve, but this is to misunderstand them. I thank them for their inspiration and for the joy their work has given me.

The designs that follow are a selection of my favorite origami toys. It has been a most pleasurable assignment to review, edit, redraw, and write about three decades of themed design work, reopening old origami documents and magazines, reviewing drawings on yellowing paper from times past, and reminiscing about treasured origami friendships, some with people no longer with me. For that, I am grateful to have had the opportunity to write this book.

READ THIS!

IF YOU ARE NEW TO ORIGAMI, or if it has been some years since you picked up an origami book, please read this section. Instead of trying to fold the most complicated models in the book without perhaps knowing the difference between a valley fold and a mountain fold, you should read carefully through these pages. They will help you enjoy your folding and ensure your success.

PAPER

Paper, of course, is essential. The absolute best paper to use for most of the toys in this book is specialist origami paper. Origami paper is square paper, colored on one side and white on the other, a little thinner than common copier paper. The difference in color between the two sides is often used to improve the recognition of a model—for example, by creating color-change eyes—rather than being used to prettify a model. Thus, the color change is often functional rather than merely decorative.

This book includes sixty pieces of origami paper for you to use. This paper will allow you to create any model in the book, except for those on pages 80, 93, 96, 99, 106, 115, and 123.

Origami paper can also be bought from a number of sources:

Stores: Try arts and crafts stores, toy stores, Japanese and East Asian stores, stationary stores, and office supply stores.

Origami societies: Most cities have an organized origami society that will sell origami paper (and books and more). To find the society local to you, simply type "origami" and your country or city name into an online search engine.

Online: Entering "origami paper" into a search engine will bring up many online retailers. You could also try auction sites for a bargain.

For those impromptu moments when you are seized by the urge to fold, or when someone suddenly requests you fold that amazing model you made last week, other papers are also suitable for folding. Try using printed junk mail—a wonderful free source of excellent paper—or magazines, old photocopies, or notepads. In truth, most papers that are printed on are okay to fold, and the potential for recycling and reusing papers in this way makes great sense in this age of increasing green awareness. Indeed, I know of origami people who on principle never buy paper to fold—they reuse papers of all kinds that others have discarded. Good for them.

Papers to avoid include newspapers, paper towels, tissue, and any other paper that will not hold a crease well.

Most origami books will rightly encourage you to fold your favorite origami masterpieces from beautiful papers and exhibit them for everyone to admire. However, the models in this book are toys, designed to be played with rather than exhibited, so it isn't at all a requirement that you hunt for that perfect sheet of Japanese handmade *washi* paper priced at six times the cost of this book. A certain snobbishness over paper for origami is generally a good thing, but it is probably unnecessary for the models in this book.

CREATING A GOOD ENVIRONMENT

There's nothing to stop you folding on your lap in front of the TV, your phone locked to your ear and the cat sitting on your head . . . but you can and should create a better environment in which to fold.

Sit at a table. Fold on a hard, smooth, clean surface. If a table is not available or if you are infirm, a large hardback book is a good substitute. Try to organize your seating arrangement so that the light is coming toward you from the front, not from directly overhead or from the sides. A frontal light source will create shadows across the folds of your paper, helping you to fold with greater accuracy and fluency. Try switching lights on or off, moving your chair, or even going to another room. Natural daylight through a window is a better source than artificial lighting. Good light is not an optional luxury, but a necessity.

Turn off your phone, switch off the TV, put the cat out, and do whatever you need to do to be able to focus on your folding. This is *your* time. We all need time to center ourselves, and doing origami is a wonderful way to achieve this.

FOLLOWING THE DRAWINGS IN THIS BOOK

Origami drawings are a language unto themselves. To fold successfully, you need to understand the instructions. Here are some tips and tricks:

Try to learn the folding symbols! When you are folding and you see a symbol you don't understand, refer to the Symbols table starting on page 9.

Fold slowly. Take your time. Don't rush. Enjoy the process of folding. You are not in a race.

Fold carefully. What one person may consider careful folding, another may consider unacceptably sloppy or unnecessarily precise, so the best advice is to fold as well as you can. Origami toys work best when the mechanisms are precisely folded, but if you are overly worried by the accuracy of what you are folding, just do what is within your capability. If precision is a problem, it will improve with practice.

Try again. From time to time, we all become stuck. To unstick yourself, first try unfolding a few steps to a point where you are sure everything is correct, and then fold forward again. Maybe you made a mistake somewhere and refolding the last few steps will solve the problem. Also, look ahead to the next step to see the shape that you are trying to achieve. If you are still stuck, put your paper down, do something else, and try again later. This often works! Remember that making origami from a book is always a challenge, and the learning curve for some people can sometimes appear steep, so an attitude of patience and cheerful perseverance is most helpful (and not just for origami!).

FOLDING YOUR PAPER

There are good and not-so-good ways to fold. Following a few simple guidelines will make your folding experience more pleasurable.

Fold away from you. When making a fold, always pick up an edge or corner near to you and fold it away from your body, making the new crease on the edge of the paper nearest to your body. Never do the opposite: never pull an edge or corner far away from you toward your body and crease across the top of the paper. You must constantly rotate the paper so that for every new fold the paper is correctly positioned. Rotate, rotate, rotate!

It is sometimes better to **fold against a hard surface** and sometimes better to fold in the air between your hands . . . but when and why? Generally, make long creases against a surface; they will be made more accurately. This usually means all the early folds. Later, when the main folds have been put in, pick up the paper and work with it between your hands. Experts like to fold entirely in the air (the "ballet of the paper" and all that), but it is better for beginners and improvers to fold against a surface.

It is worth remembering that origami is not just a folded art, but a folding art; that is, **the process of folding should be enjoyable,** not just a means to an end, to be rushed through as quickly as possible on the way to making a model. Think of folding as a gourmet meal, whose delicate and diverse flavors and many courses should be savored slowly. Folding should not be like gobbling down a drive-in take-away and speeding off. Following the above advice will make your folding experience pleasurable, not a chore, and you will want to do more. The art of origami should be a sensual experience, never just a mechanical means to an end.

WHAT TO DO WITH YOUR ORIGAMI TOYS

In two words . . . share them!

Of all origami genres, toys should be shared. Learn a few of your favorites by heart and make them for family and friends, or as icebreakers with strangers at parties, dreary meetings, long flights, and the like. A designer friend once told me how she traveled from remote village to remote village in several Southeast Asian countries on a research project, gaining the friendship and help of the villagers by folding origami toys for everyone!

If you have the confidence, teach origami toys to club groups, young or old. They are great to teach to children, who love to play with them; adults love them too. Some of my most enjoyable workshops have been with groups as diverse as graphic design students at a design college in central London, a group of engineering professionals, a group of elderly ladies, and a small class of children at a rural village deep in the English countryside.

If you are a teacher, teach origami toys in class as a fun end-of-semester treat, or more seriously in math, science, and technology classes (there are some great examples of levers and other mechanisms contained in the toys). Teaching toys to disruptive children gives them status and self-confidence, or they can be given as rewards for good behavior. I know of therapists who gain the trust of children by making origami toys for them and who use mouth toys in role-playing games.

The essence of an origami toy is its innocent delight. But presented in the right way at the right time, a toy may also have a serious educational or therapeutic use. Don't confuse fun with triviality!

SYMBOLS

It's not so much the step-by-step drawings themselves as the symbols superimposed on them that tell you how to make an origami model. Over the years, a general consensus has been unofficially agreed upon between origami authors of many countries and different languages to make the symbols universal. This means—in theory, anyway—that paper folders around the world can pick up any origami book and be able to make the models it contains because the symbols are broadly the same, book to book and language to language. The symbols included in this book are not the complete set used worldwide, but they are sufficient to enable you to make the models it contains.

With two exceptions, the symbols are largely self-explanatory. The exceptions are the symbols for the two basic folds of valley fold and mountain fold (actually, if you think about it, they are the same fold). Each folding symbol should be learned before you begin this book.

Mountain Fold and Valley Fold: 3D

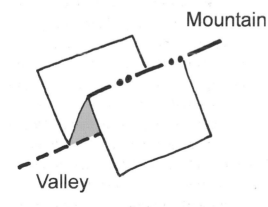

Valley fold

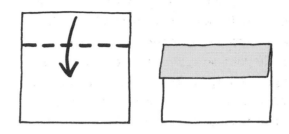

Mountain fold

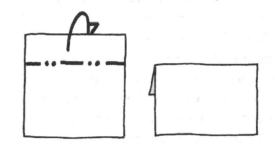

Existing fold

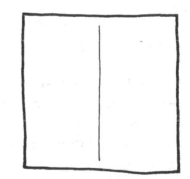

Fold and open

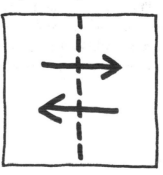

X-ray view or tuck in

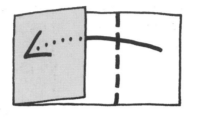

Turn over

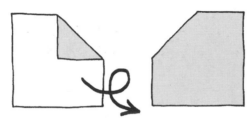

Fold dot to dot

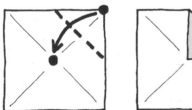

TECHNIQUES

Valley folds and mountain folds are simply "folds." That is, one new fold is made at a time, either by bringing part of the paper toward you (to make a valley fold) or turning it away from you (to make a mountain fold), and then flattening it to make a new crease. That's really all there is to say about valley and mountain folding.

However, there are more complex techniques in which a number of new folds are made simultaneously. These techniques are important because they hugely increase the possible number of folded shapes, and thus they increase perhaps almost to infinity the number of models that can be made.

There are many advanced manipulation techniques (Squash, Sink, Rabbit Ear, Petal Fold, etc.), but the most common techniques are the Inside Reverse Fold and its less common complementary, the Outside Reverse Fold. Once learned, these are very quick and simple to make, but at first sight they can seem difficult to understand. If you are unfamiliar with these techniques, I strongly recommend that you make the examples that follow, rather than trying to fold them for the first time when making a model.

INSIDE REVERSE FOLD

This is so-called because the part of the paper that is manipulated reverses inside the remainder of the paper.

1. Begin with a square, white side up. Fold in half along a diagonal and unfold.

2. Fold the top left and top right edges to the center line.

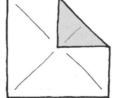

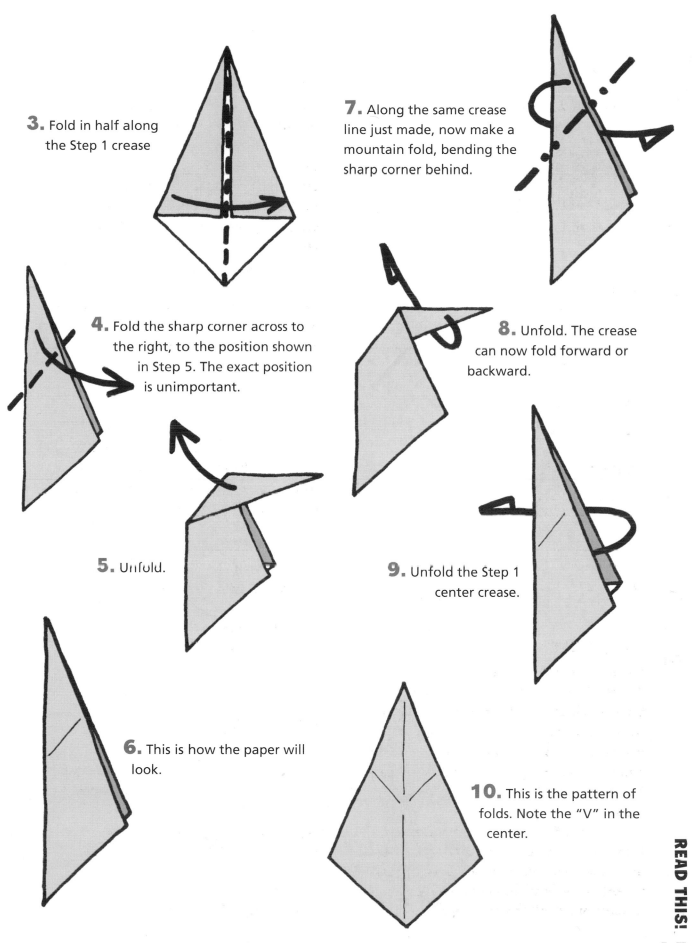

3. Fold in half along the Step 1 crease

4. Fold the sharp corner across to the right, to the position shown in Step 5. The exact position is unimportant.

5. Unfold.

6. This is how the paper will look.

7. Along the same crease line just made, now make a mountain fold, bending the sharp corner behind.

8. Unfold. The crease can now fold forward or backward.

9. Unfold the Step 1 center crease.

10. This is the pattern of folds. Note the "V" in the center.

11. Think of the paper as having four folds that all meet at the bottom of the "V." From this side of the paper, three of those folds will be mountains, and one will be a valley. If you make these four folds one at a time and then collapse all the creases simultaneously, you can jump straight to the end, at Step 16, but it is more instructive to follow the method in Steps 12–15.

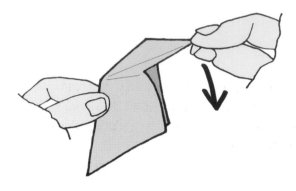

14. . . . like this. Allow the "V" fold to form. Make the valley fold seen in Step 11, so that the paper will begin to flatten itself . . .

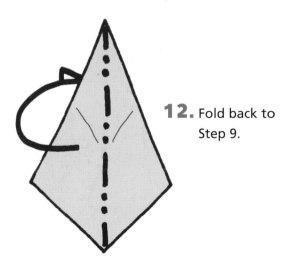

12. Fold back to Step 9.

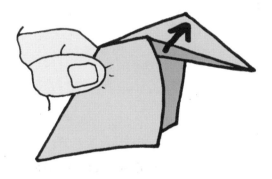

15. . . . like this. Continue to flatten the paper . . .

13. Hold the paper as shown between your two hands. Begin to move the sharp corner downward and—crucially—down through the middle of the paper, between the front and back sides . . .

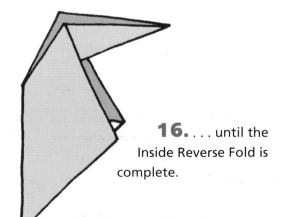

16. . . . until the Inside Reverse Fold is complete.

INSIDE REVERSE FOLDS IN THE BOOK

The explanation above took many steps, too many to be repeated again and again in the book. So here is how the book explains what you have just done.

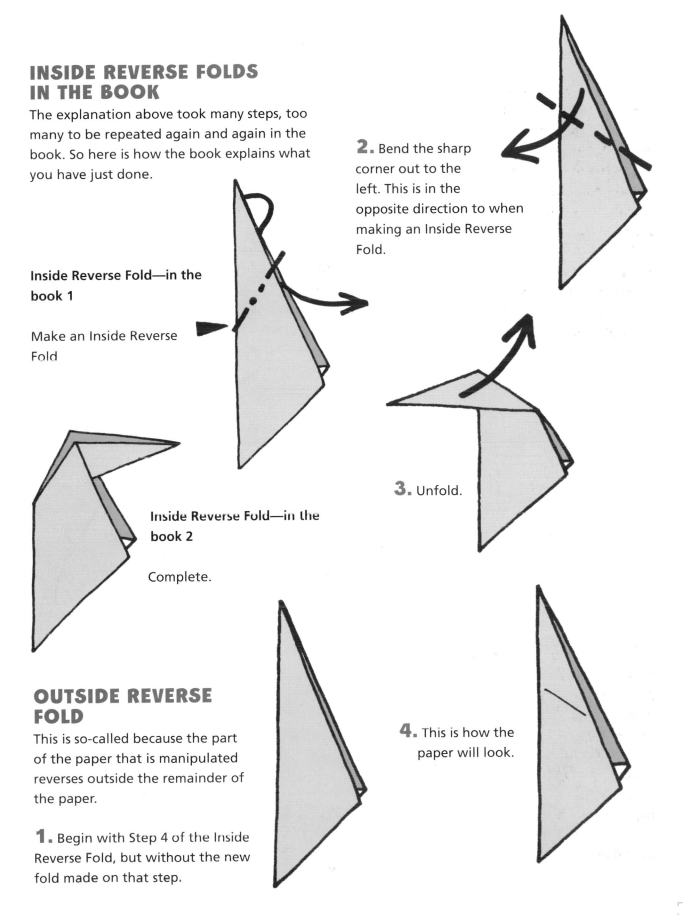

Inside Reverse Fold—in the book 1

Make an Inside Reverse Fold

Inside Reverse Fold—in the book 2

Complete.

2. Bend the sharp corner out to the left. This is in the opposite direction to when making an Inside Reverse Fold.

3. Unfold.

OUTSIDE REVERSE FOLD

This is so-called because the part of the paper that is manipulated reverses outside the remainder of the paper.

1. Begin with Step 4 of the Inside Reverse Fold, but without the new fold made on that step.

4. This is how the paper will look.

5. Along the same crease line just made, now make a mountain fold, bending the sharp corner behind.

6. Unfold. The crease can now fold forward or backward.

7. Swing the back layer around to the left.

8. This is the pattern of folds. Note the upturned "V" in the center. Note too how this pattern differs from the Inside Reverse Fold.

9. Think of the paper as having four folds that all meet at the top of the upturned "V." From this side of the paper, three of those folds will be valleys, and one will be a mountain. Note how the number of valleys and mountains is reversed compared to the Inside Reverse Fold. If you make these four folds one at a time and then collapse all the creases simultaneously, you can jump straight to the end, at Step 12, but it is more instructive to follow the method in Steps 10–11.

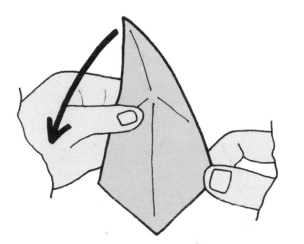

10. Hold the paper as shown. Bend the sharp corner forward, simultaneously folding the paper in half down the middle and allowing the valley folds of the upturned "V" to form . . .

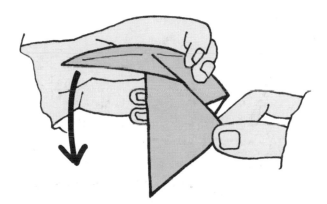

11. . . . like this. For a while the paper will be curvy, so encourage it to flatten . . .

12. . . . until the Outside Reverse Fold is complete.

OUTSIDE REVERSE FOLDS IN THE BOOK

The explanation above took many steps, too many to be repeated again and again in the book. So here is how the book explains what you have just done.

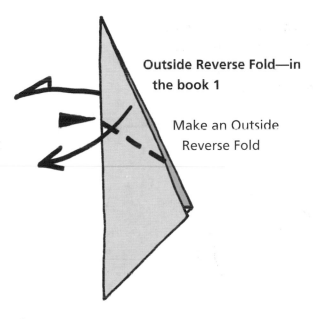

Outside Reverse Fold—in the book 1

Make an Outside Reverse Fold

Outside Reverse Fold—in the book 2

Complete.

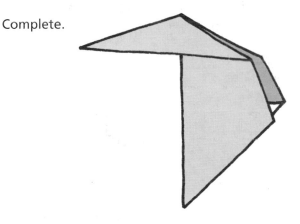

PECKING BIRD

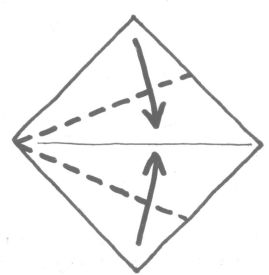

I remember sitting at a kitchen table, talking to friends and playing idly with a square of paper . . . and suddenly, there was the completed Pecking Bird in my hand, hungrily eating its imaginary food! If I had been trying to make it, I would never have succeeded.

Begin with a square of origami paper, white side up.

1. Fold corner to corner. Unfold.

2. Fold the top left and bottom left edges of the paper square to the center line.

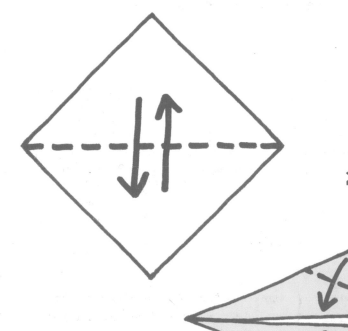

3. Similarly, fold the top right and bottom right edges also to the center line, eliminating all the white paper from view.

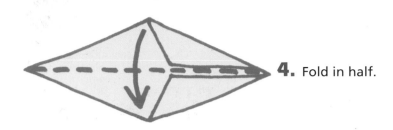

4. Fold in half.

5. Make an Inside Reverse Fold (see page 10). Look at Step 6 to see the final position of the paper. Note how the sharp corner protrudes a little.

6. Now make an Outside Reverse Fold (see page 13). Look at Step 7 to see the final position of the paper after the fold has been made.

7. Draw an eye (and a beak, wings, and whatever else takes your fancy.)

8. Grip the tip of the Inside Reverse Fold between your thumb and middle finger. Rest the bottom corners of the bird on a smooth surface. Depress the top edge of the reverse fold with your first finger . . .

9. . . . like this. The reverse fold will flatten and the bird will peck the ground in front of it! The action is large and smooth, but if it doesn't work too well the first time, move your hand around on the paper to find the best positions for your finger and thumb.

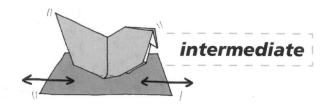
FEEDING BIRD

This model is a variation on a classic design by Seiryo Takekawa, but is made very differently. My design is higher and less stable than his, so it rocks back and forth with more energy . . . but it can also fall over if the rocking is too vigorous. The critical folds are at Step 12.

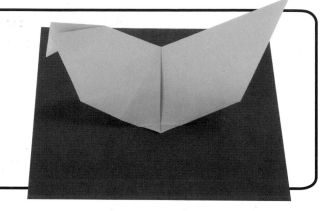

Begin with a square of origami paper, white side up.

1. Fold the bottom corner up to the top corner.

2. Fold the triangle in half.

3. Unfold the paper completely.

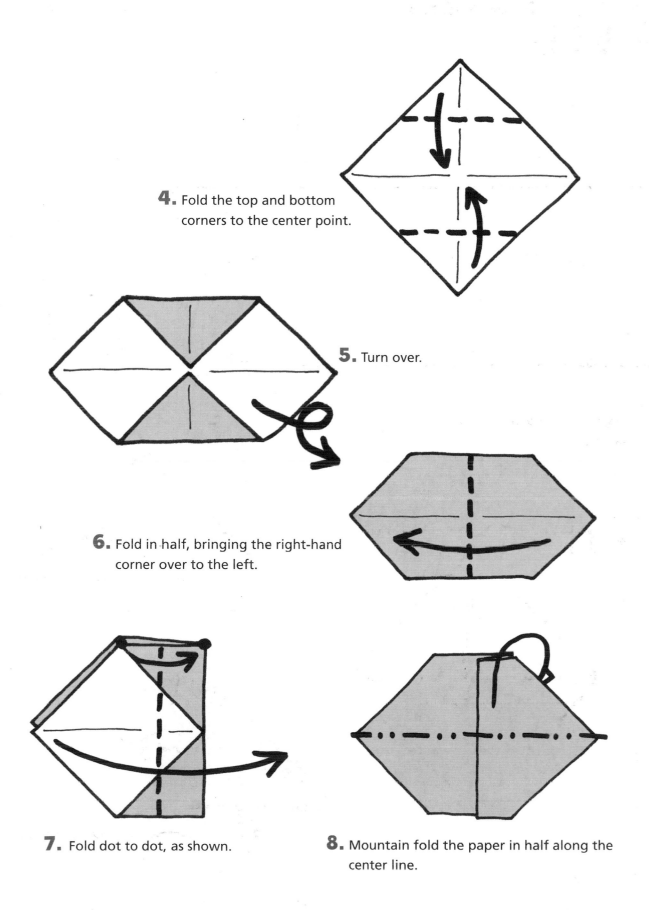

4. Fold the top and bottom corners to the center point.

5. Turn over.

6. Fold in half, bringing the right-hand corner over to the left.

7. Fold dot to dot, as shown.

8. Mountain fold the paper in half along the center line.

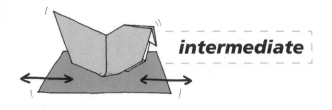

9. Hold the paper as shown in your two hands. Move your right hand up and to the right. The paper will swivel open . . .

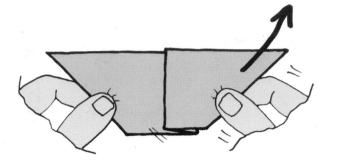

10. . . . like this. Flatten the paper, making a new crease as shown. Take care to make a neat corner at the bottom end of the new fold.

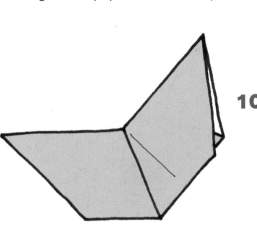

11. Make an Inside Reverse Fold (see page 10). Look at Step 12 for the position of the fold.

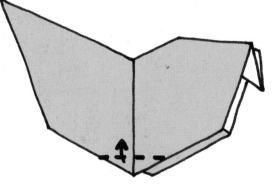

12. Fold up the bottom corner just a little, front and back. The length of this fold is critical. Make it too long or too short and the bird will not rock well. The first time you fold this model, take a little time to experiment with its exact length.

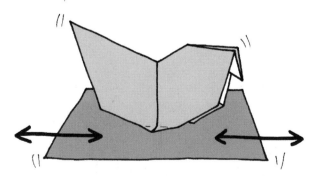

13. To make the bird feed, place it on an unfolded square of origami paper. Move the square left and right and the bird will rock back and forth! If the action is unconvincing, adjust the all-important Step 12 folds.

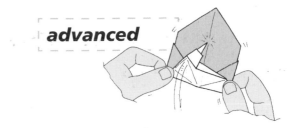

WOODPECKER

If the pecking of your bird is very quiet, try moving your thumbs and fingers around on the paper and moving your hands apart and together with a different rhythm and motion. With practice, the noise will be surprisingly loud.

Begin with a square of origami paper, colored side up.

1. Fold corner to corner. Unfold.

2. Bring the bottom edges of the paper square to the center line.

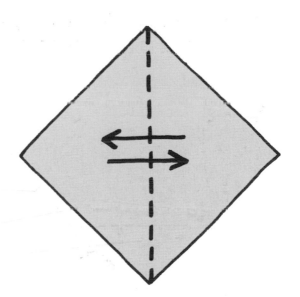

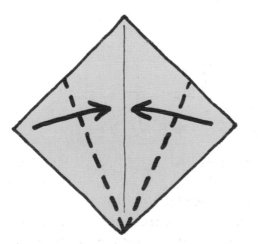

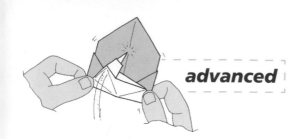

advanced

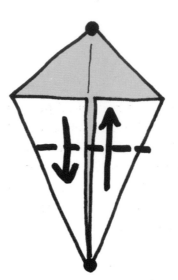

3. Fold dot to dot. Unfold.

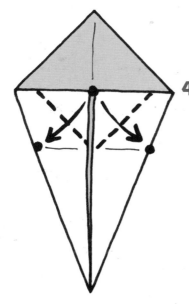

4. Fold dot to dot, exposing two colored triangles.

5. With mountain folds, fold behind the excess paper at the left and right. Note that the folds are parallel to the center line.

6. Fold the paper in half.

WOODPECKER — *advanced*

22

7. Rotate the paper to a horizontal position. We are about to make two folds, so that the paper looks like Step 9 when finished. The mountain fold already exists. The angled valley fold is new. When the two folds are made together, on the front and back of the paper, it will look . . .

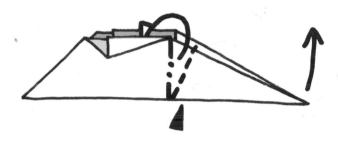

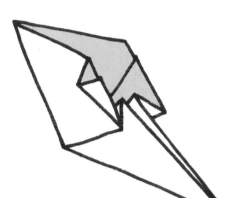

8. . . . like this. The technical description is a "crimp." Flatten the paper so that it looks exactly like Step 9.

9. This is the completed crimp. Now make an Outside Reverse Fold (see page 13) that begins deep inside the crimp and slopes up a little as it moves to the right . . .

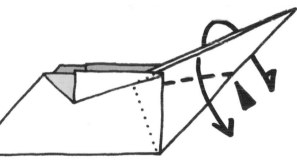

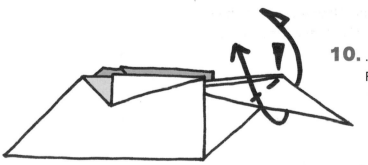

10. . . . like this. Make another Outside Reverse Fold . . .

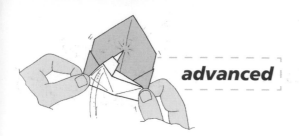

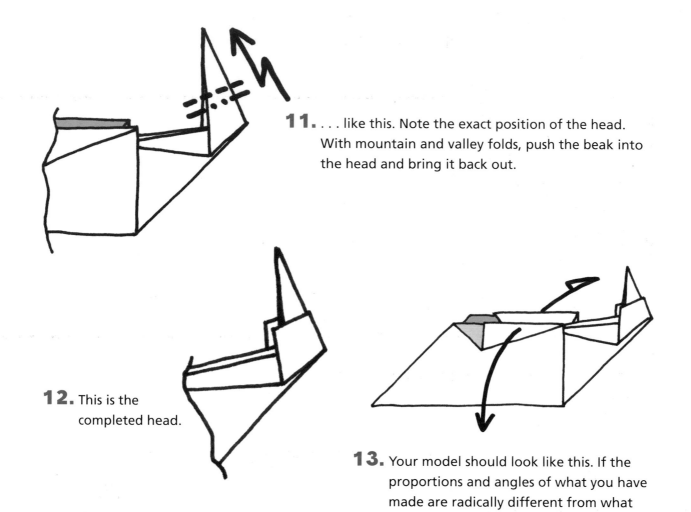

11. . . . like this. Note the exact position of the head. With mountain and valley folds, push the beak into the head and bring it back out.

12. This is the completed head.

13. Your model should look like this. If the proportions and angles of what you have made are radically different from what is shown here, start again from Step 7. Open the center fold of the paper.

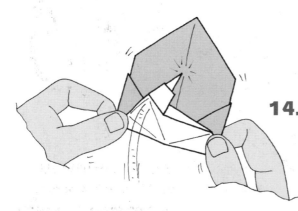

14. To make a loud "rat-a-tat" sound, hold very firmly as shown. Your thumbs are just below the V-shaped valley fold made in Step 7. Move your hands rapidly together and apart and the head should knock noisily against the tree!

SQUAWKING BIRD

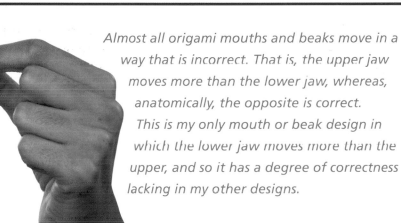

Almost all origami mouths and beaks move in a way that is incorrect. That is, the upper jaw moves more than the lower jaw, whereas, anatomically, the opposite is correct.
This is my only mouth or beak design in which the lower jaw moves more than the upper, and so it has a degree of correctness lacking in my other designs.

Begin with a square of origami paper, white side up.

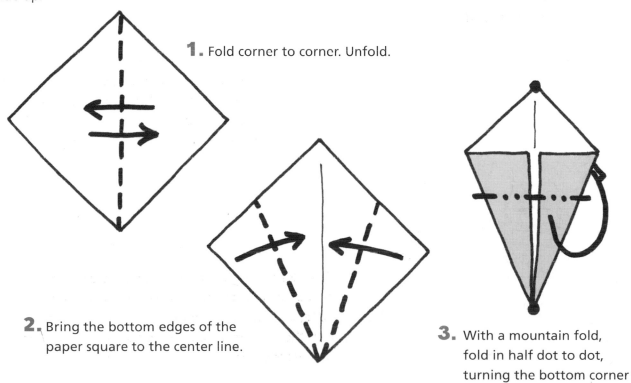

1. Fold corner to corner. Unfold.

2. Bring the bottom edges of the paper square to the center line.

3. With a mountain fold, fold in half dot to dot, turning the bottom corner behind.

intermediate

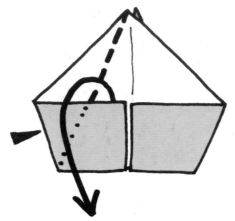

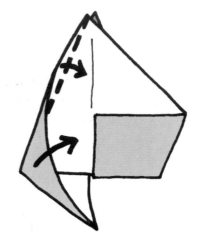

4. Apply pressure to the short folded edge at the left, opening the pocket behind the colored paper . . .

5. . . . like this. Gradually flatten the paper, making a long sloping crease up to the top corner of the paper . . .

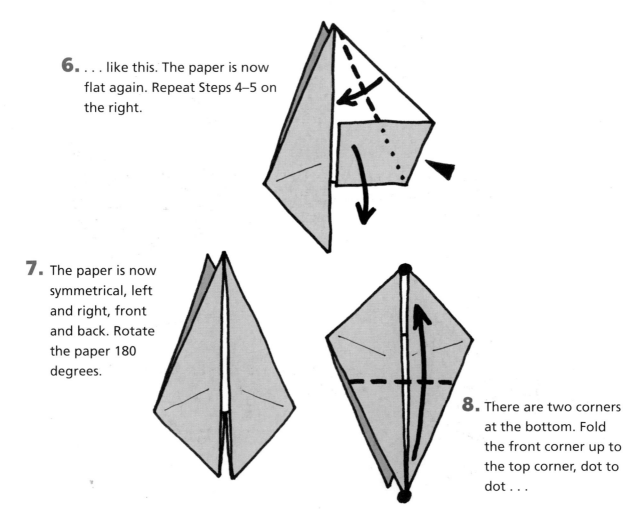

6. . . . like this. The paper is now flat again. Repeat Steps 4–5 on the right.

7. The paper is now symmetrical, left and right, front and back. Rotate the paper 180 degrees.

8. There are two corners at the bottom. Fold the front corner up to the top corner, dot to dot . . .

SQUAWKING BIRD — *intermediate*

9. . . . like this. Fold down the left edge of the triangle to lie along the bottom edge, bisecting the angle, as shown. Look at Step 10.

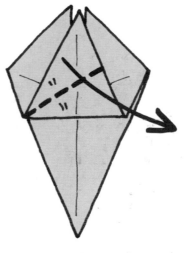

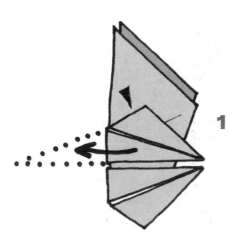

10. Repeat Step 9 with the bottom triangle . . .

11. . . . like this. Mountain fold the entire left side of the paper behind the right side.

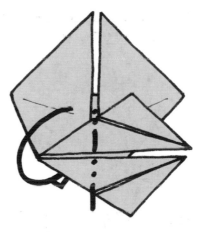

12. Swing the upper loose point over to the left, flattening the paper.

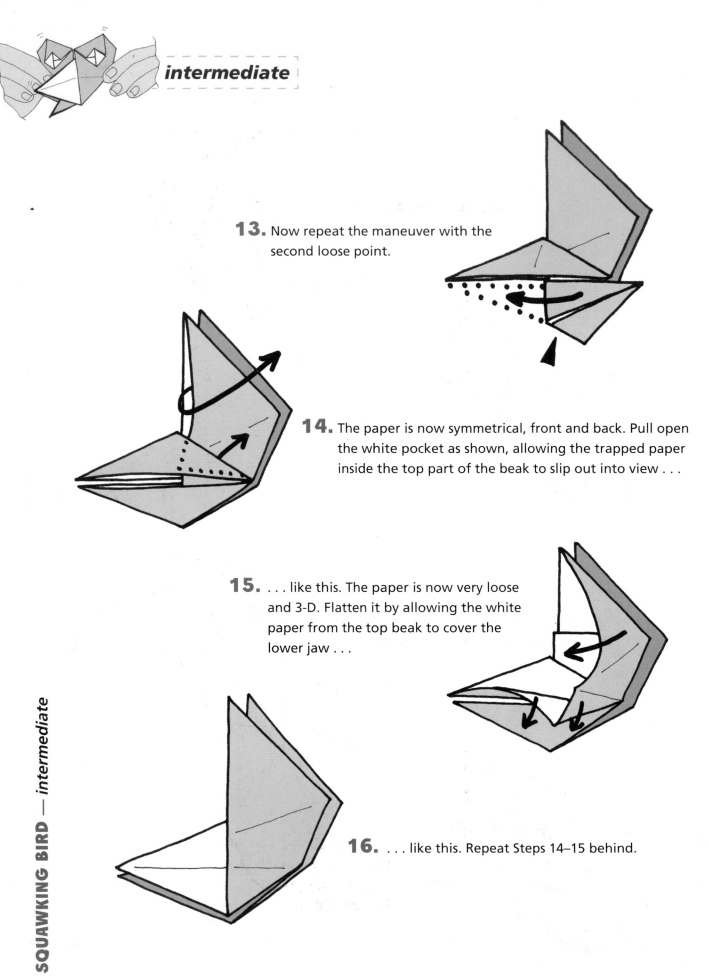

13. Now repeat the maneuver with the second loose point.

14. The paper is now symmetrical, front and back. Pull open the white pocket as shown, allowing the trapped paper inside the top part of the beak to slip out into view . . .

15. . . . like this. The paper is now very loose and 3-D. Flatten it by allowing the white paper from the top beak to cover the lower jaw . . .

16. . . . like this. Repeat Steps 14–15 behind.

17. Fold dot to dot. Repeat behind.

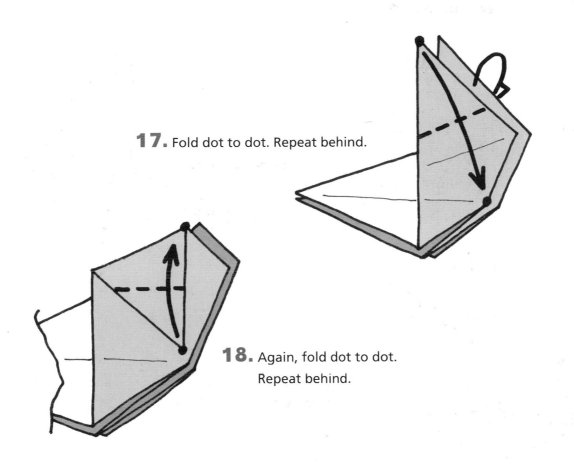

18. Again, fold dot to dot.
Repeat behind.

19. Apply pressure on the folded edge,
opening the white pocket and squashing
the pocket flat . . .

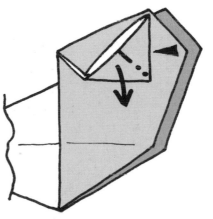

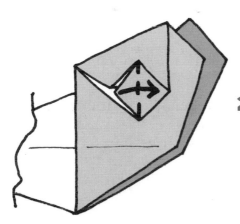

20. . . . like this. Repeat behind.
Fold the corner across to the
right, exposing white paper.
Repeat behind.

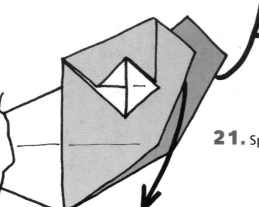

21. Spread apart the two sides of the head.

22. Make a valley fold as shown, thus enabling the lower jaw to swivel 180 degrees backward . . .

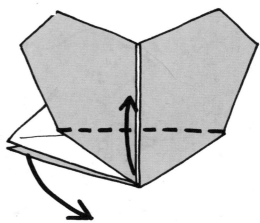

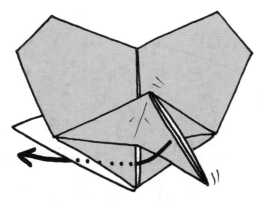

23. . . . like this. When the fold has been made, unfold Step 22 to return the lower jaw to its correct position.

24. Hold as shown. By moving your hands back and forth, the lower jaw will move up and down.

FLAPPING BIRD 1

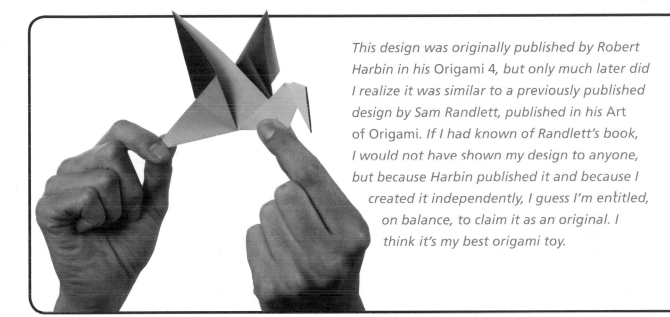

This design was originally published by Robert Harbin in his Origami 4, but only much later did I realize it was similar to a previously published design by Sam Randlett, published in his Art of Origami. If I had known of Randlett's book, I would not have shown my design to anyone, but because Harbin published it and because I created it independently, I guess I'm entitled, on balance, to claim it as an original. I think it's my best origami toy.

Begin with a square of origami paper, white side up.

1. Fold corner to corner. Unfold.

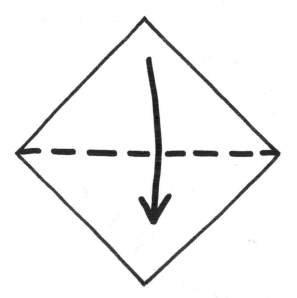

2. Fold down the middle. Unfold.

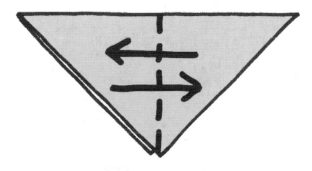

3. On the right side only, fold the right-hand corner down to the bottom corner.

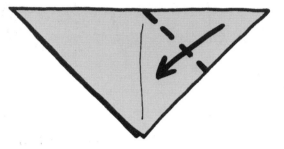

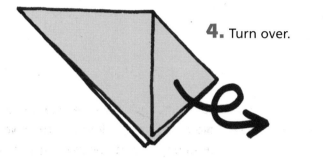

4. Turn over.

5. Repeat Step 3, folding the right-hand corner down to the bottom corner.

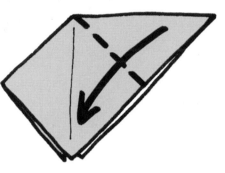

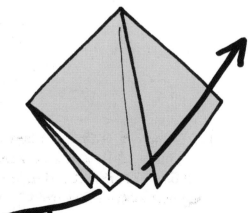

6. There are now four loose corners at the bottom corner. Begin to separate them, pulling the two front corners forward, exposing white paper inside . . .

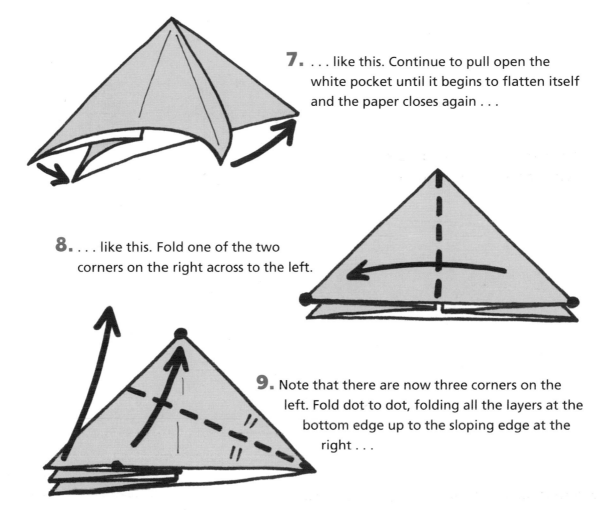

7. . . . like this. Continue to pull open the white pocket until it begins to flatten itself and the paper closes again . . .

8. . . . like this. Fold one of the two corners on the right across to the left.

9. Note that there are now three corners on the left. Fold dot to dot, folding all the layers at the bottom edge up to the sloping edge at the right . . .

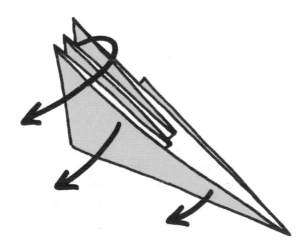

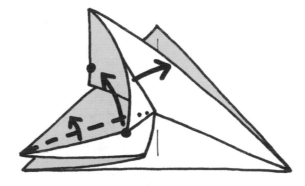

10. . . . like this. Of the three corners now at the top, pull the front two back down . . .

11. . . . like this. The paper is now very 3-D and unresolved. Flatten the paper as shown, folding dot to dot. Note that almost all the visible paper is now white.

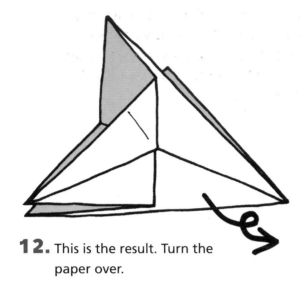

12. This is the result. Turn the paper over.

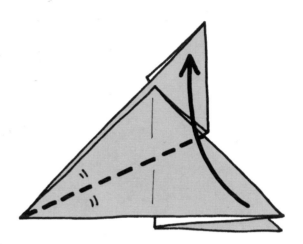

13. Fold the paper in half . . .

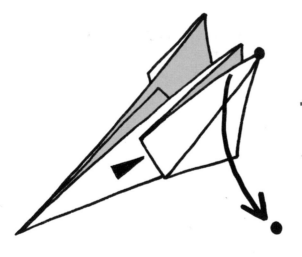

14. . . . like this. Pull down just the front (white) corner, allowing the paper to once again become 3-D and unresolved . . .

15. . . . like this. Flatten the paper with a crease to the bottom right corner.

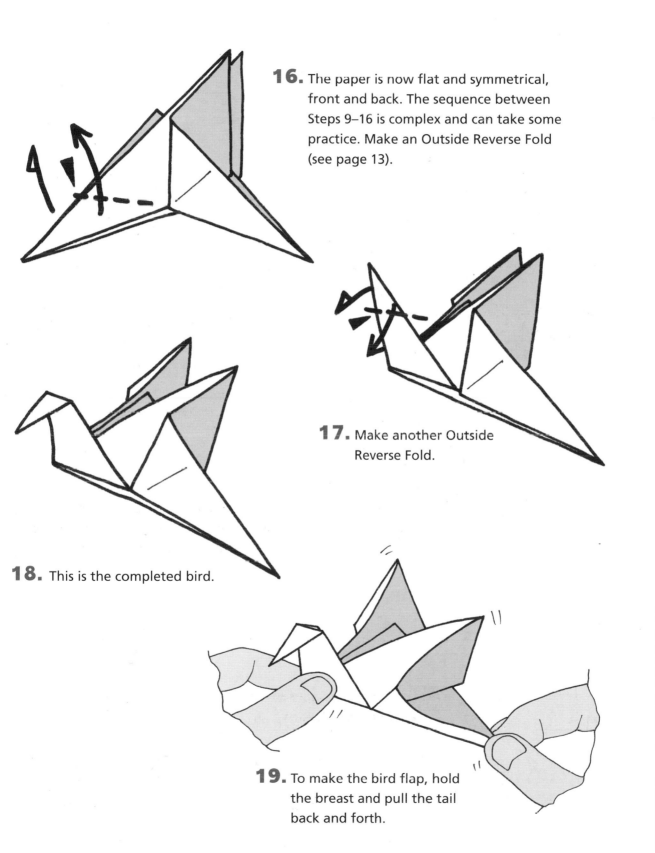

16. The paper is now flat and symmetrical, front and back. The sequence between Steps 9–16 is complex and can take some practice. Make an Outside Reverse Fold (see page 13).

17. Make another Outside Reverse Fold.

18. This is the completed bird.

19. To make the bird flap, hold the breast and pull the tail back and forth.

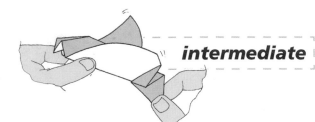

FLAPPING BIRD 2

This is my attempt to create a flapping bird with a good action, which has a very simple and direct folding sequence. There are some simpler flapping birds out there, but in my opinion they are wigglers, not flappers.

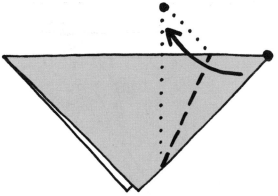

Begin with a square of origami paper, white side up.

1. Fold in half, corner to corner.

2. Fold dot to dot, as shown.

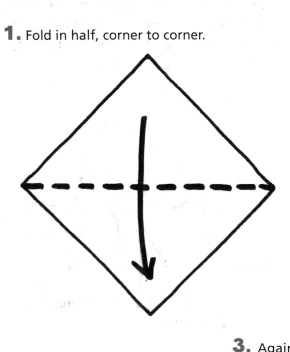

3. Again, fold dot to dot.

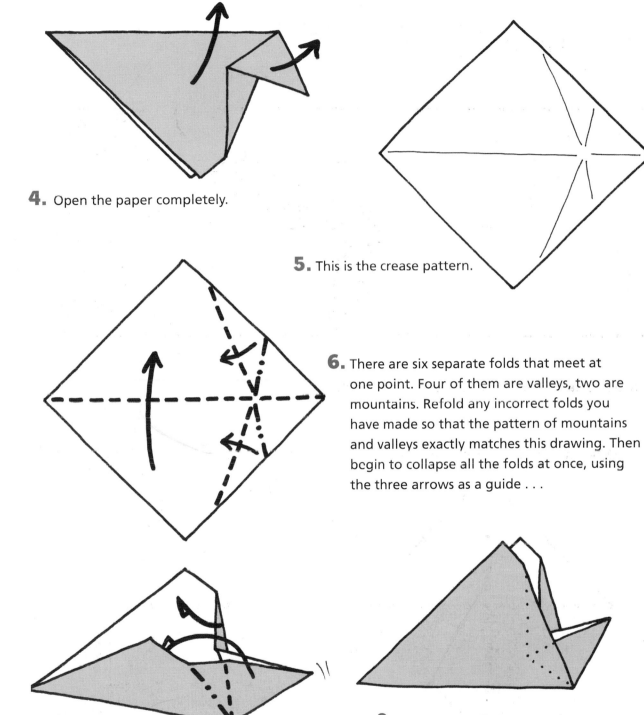

4. Open the paper completely.

5. This is the crease pattern.

6. There are six separate folds that meet at one point. Four of them are valleys, two are mountains. Refold any incorrect folds you have made so that the pattern of mountains and valleys exactly matches this drawing. Then begin to collapse all the folds at once, using the three arrows as a guide . . .

7. . . . like this. The paper is seen here half collapsed. Continue to collapse the paper . . .

8. . . . until it is flat. Rotate the paper 180 degrees.

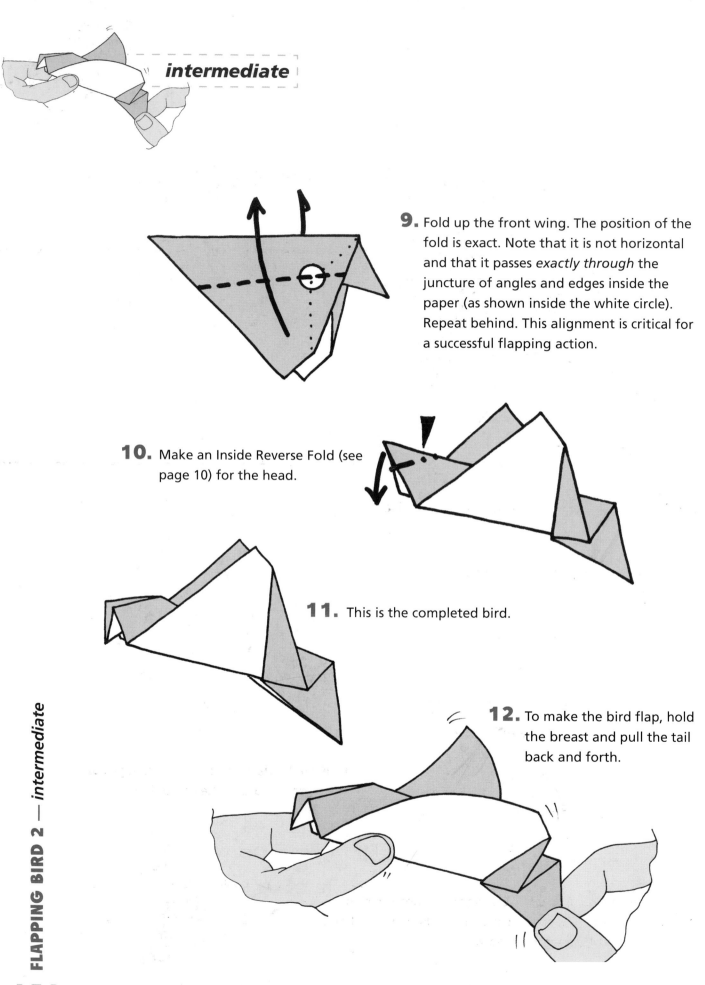

9. Fold up the front wing. The position of the fold is exact. Note that it is not horizontal and that it passes *exactly through* the juncture of angles and edges inside the paper (as shown inside the white circle). Repeat behind. This alignment is critical for a successful flapping action.

10. Make an Inside Reverse Fold (see page 10) for the head.

11. This is the completed bird.

12. To make the bird flap, hold the breast and pull the tail back and forth.

SNAPPING CROCODILE 1

If you experiment with the folding of the crocodile's eyes, many variations can be made. The shape of the snout can change too.

Begin with a square of origami paper, colored side up.

1. Fold and unfold corner to corner. Turn over.

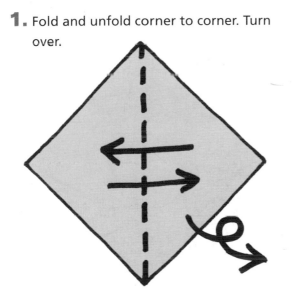

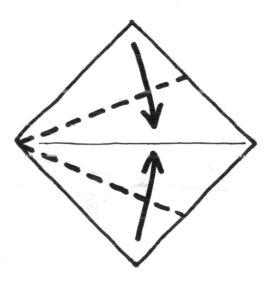

2. Fold the top left and bottom left edges of the paper square to the center line.

3. Similarly, fold the top right and bottom right edges also to the center line, eliminating all the white paper from view.

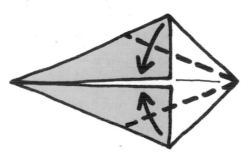

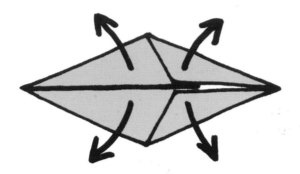

4. Unfold the paper back to Step 1.

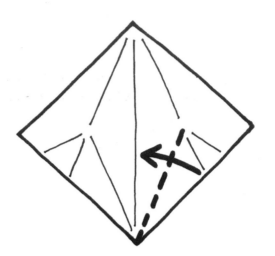

5. Rotate the paper to the position shown. Fold just the single valley fold as shown . . .

6. . . . like this. On the colored triangle, make the mountain and valley folds as shown. These folds will collapse the paper flat . . .

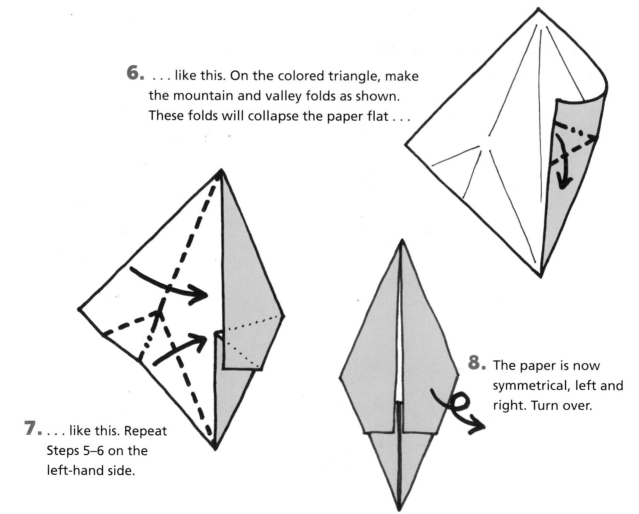

7. . . . like this. Repeat Steps 5–6 on the left-hand side.

8. The paper is now symmetrical, left and right. Turn over.

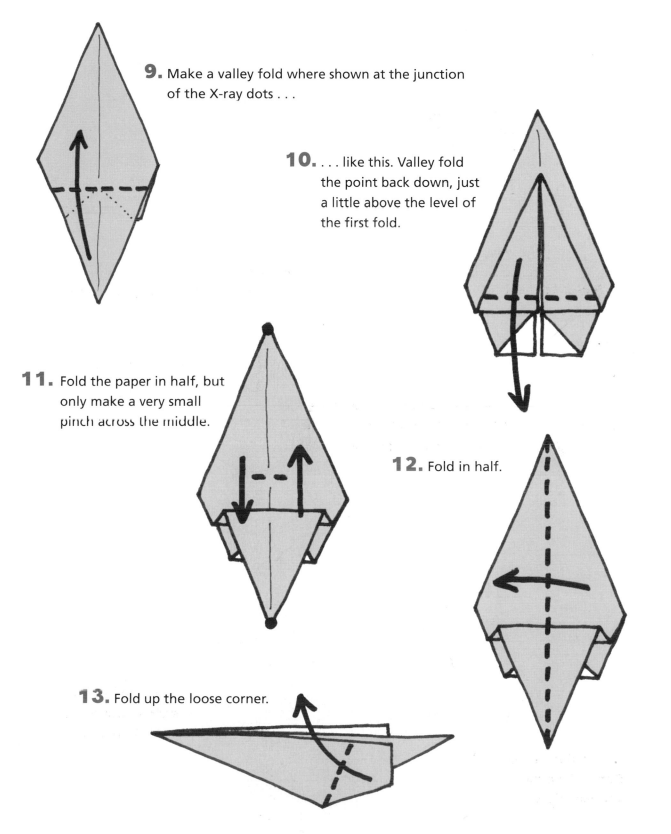

9. Make a valley fold where shown at the junction of the X-ray dots . . .

10. . . . like this. Valley fold the point back down, just a little above the level of the first fold.

11. Fold the paper in half, but only make a very small pinch across the middle.

12. Fold in half.

13. Fold up the loose corner.

14. Fold dot to dot.

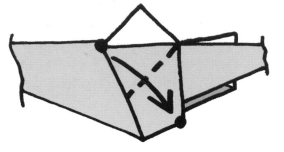

15. Again, fold dot to dot.

16. And finally, fold again dot to dot.

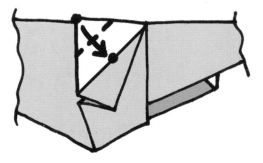

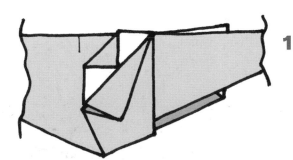

17. This is how the eye should look. Make the other eye by repeating Steps 13–16 on the back.

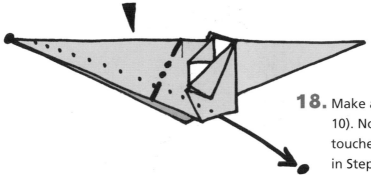

18. Make an Inside Reverse Fold (see page 10). Note that the top of the fold touches the midway pinch made back in Step 11.

19. Pull out the eye assembly so that both eyes stand out at right angles to the plane of the head . . .

20. . . . like this. Note how this makes the eyes look forward, down the line of the snout.

21. To make the crocodile snap, hold as shown. The first finger is behind the eyes and the thumb is up inside the lower jaw.

SNAPPING CROCODILE 2

The mechanism here is very different from that of the Snapping Crocodile 1, being geometrically more sophisticated. This same mechanism is used in the Lip Smacker (see page 96). With only a small movement of the finger and thumb, the jaws will open and close considerably.

Begin with a square of origami paper folded to Step 8 of Snapping Crocodile 1.

1. Turn over.

2. Fold dot to dot, but only make a small pinch across the center line.

3. Make the short valley fold as shown . . .

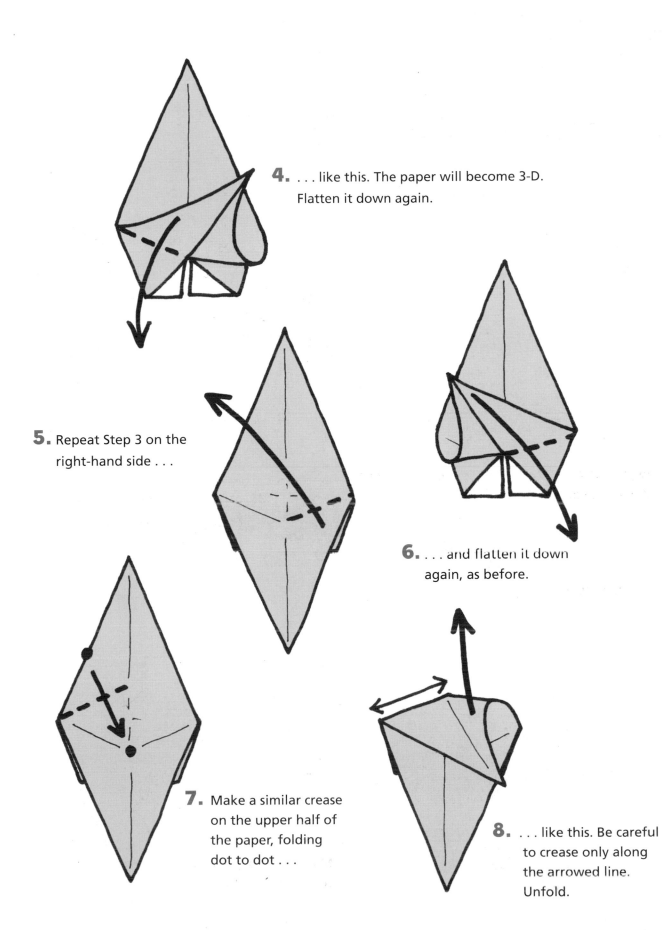

4. . . . like this. The paper will become 3-D. Flatten it down again.

5. Repeat Step 3 on the right-hand side . . .

6. . . . and flatten it down again, as before.

7. Make a similar crease on the upper half of the paper, folding dot to dot . . .

8. . . . like this. Be careful to crease only along the arrowed line. Unfold.

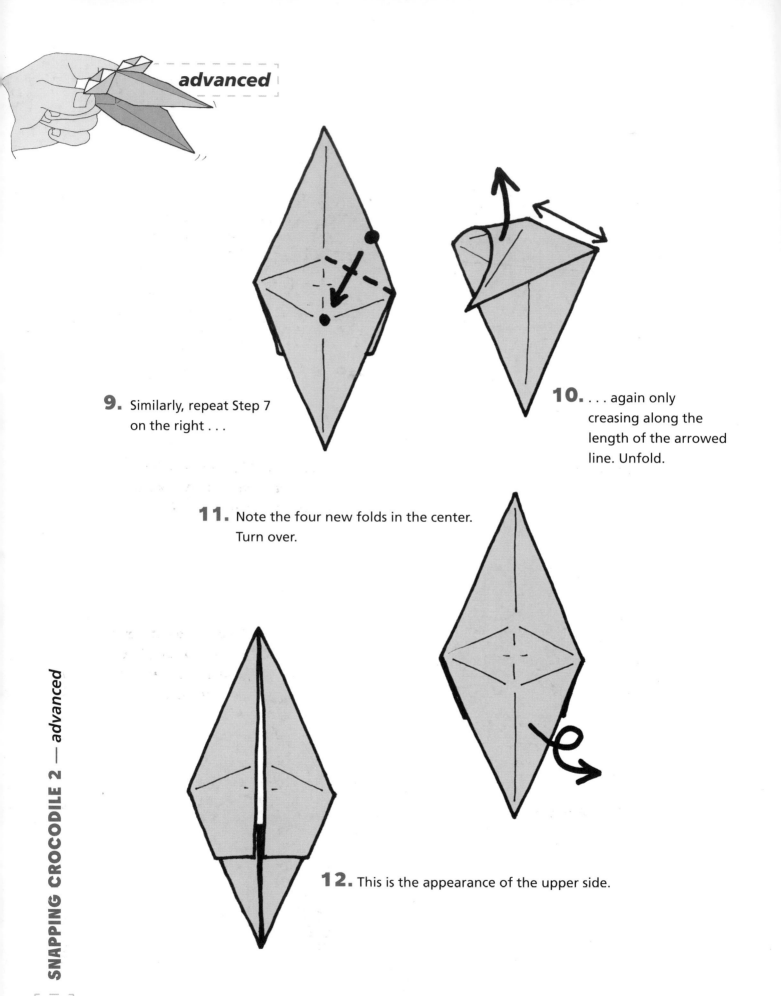

9. Similarly, repeat Step 7 on the right . . .

10. . . . again only creasing along the length of the arrowed line. Unfold.

11. Note the four new folds in the center. Turn over.

12. This is the appearance of the upper side.

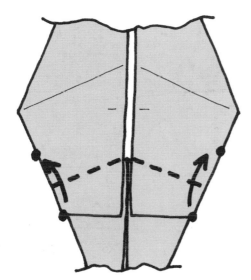

13. Fold dot to dot . . .

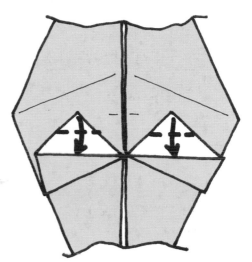

14. . . . like this. Note how the white triangles look. Fold the white triangles in half.

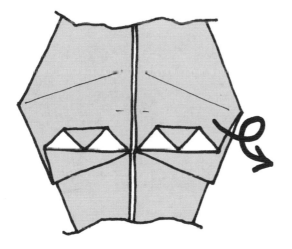

15. Turn over.

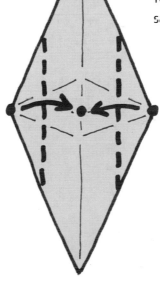

16. Fold dot to dot, being careful to make both folds parallel and the same length.

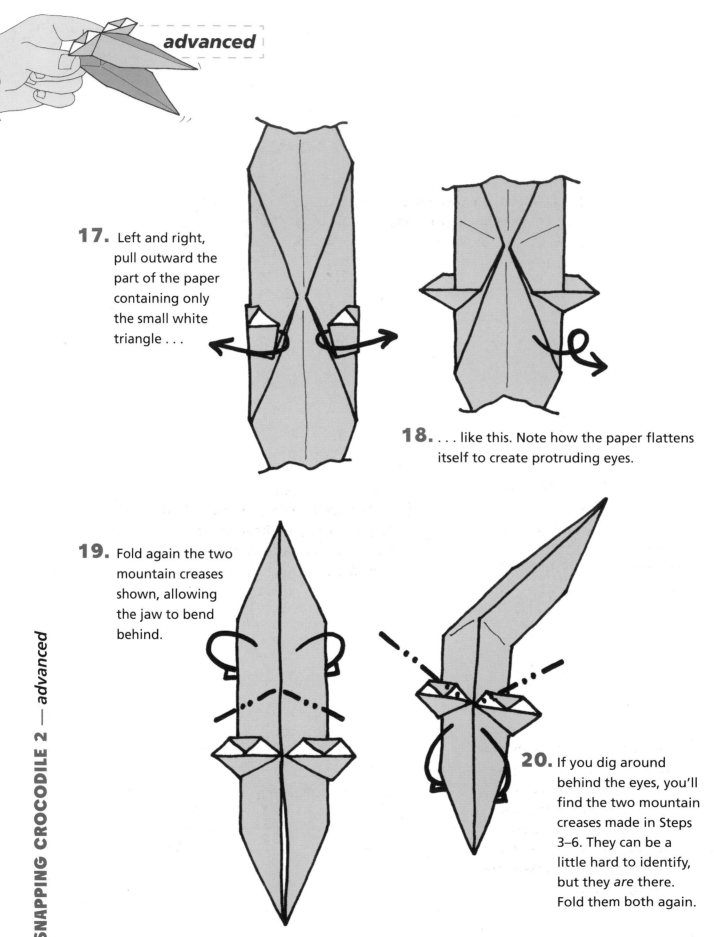

17. Left and right, pull outward the part of the paper containing only the small white triangle . . .

18. . . . like this. Note how the paper flattens itself to create protruding eyes.

19. Fold again the two mountain creases shown, allowing the jaw to bend behind.

20. If you dig around behind the eyes, you'll find the two mountain creases made in Steps 3–6. They can be a little hard to identify, but they *are* there. Fold them both again.

SNAPPING CROCODILE 2 — *advanced*

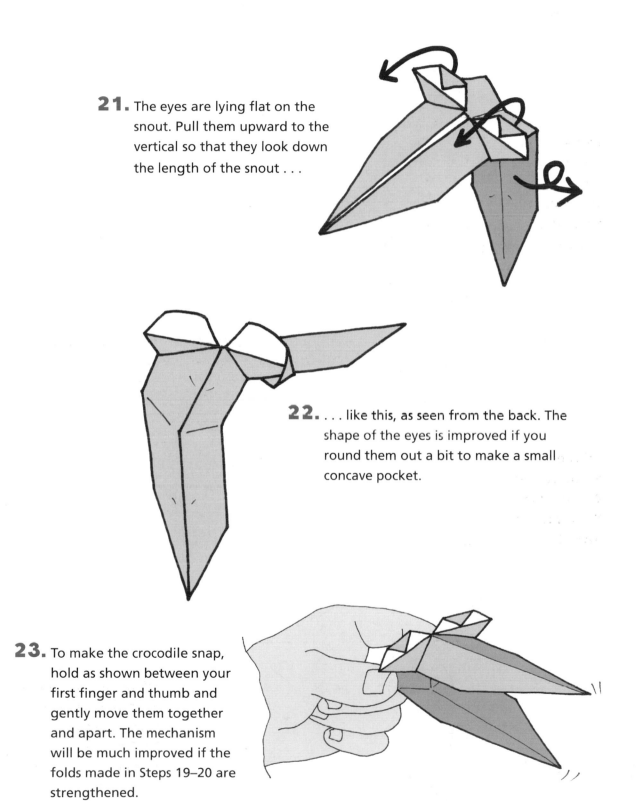

21. The eyes are lying flat on the snout. Pull them upward to the vertical so that they look down the length of the snout . . .

22. . . . like this, as seen from the back. The shape of the eyes is improved if you round them out a bit to make a small concave pocket.

23. To make the crocodile snap, hold as shown between your first finger and thumb and gently move them together and apart. The mechanism will be much improved if the folds made in Steps 19–20 are strengthened.

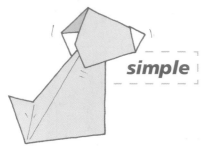

simple

NODDING DOG

My goal with this model was to create a design with as few folds as possible. This extreme simplicity poses its own challenges.

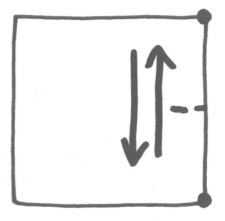

Begin with two squares of origami paper, white side up. The first step shows the relative sizes of the squares.

Use two squares of the same color. Cut the Head square so that it is roughly two-thirds the size of the Body square.

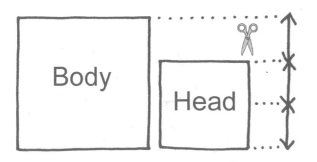

BODY

1. With the Body square, bring two adjacent corners together and pinch the edge of the paper at the right.

2. Fold dot to dot, as shown, so that the bottom left corner lies on the pinch and the new fold starts at the top left-hand corner of the square . . .

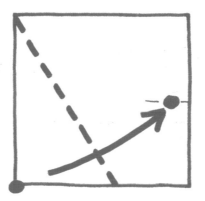

3. . . . like this. The top right-hand corner will now fold exactly over the colored triangle.

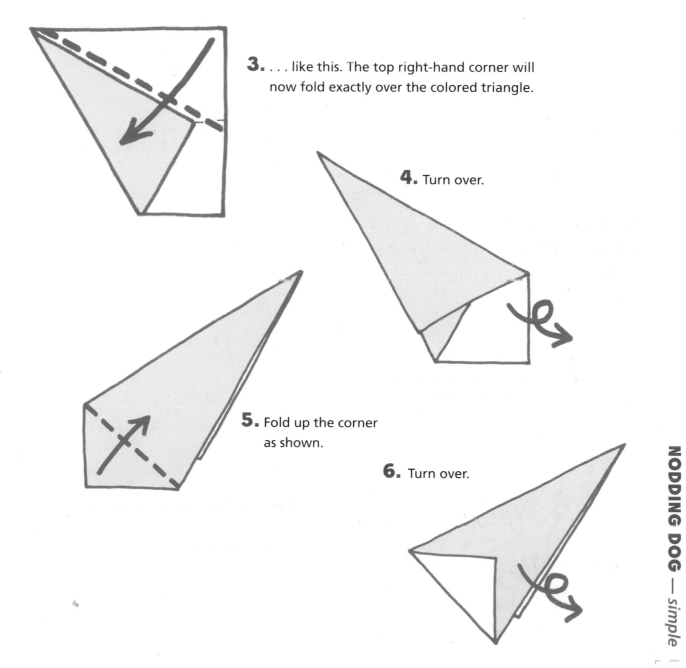

4. Turn over.

5. Fold up the corner as shown.

6. Turn over.

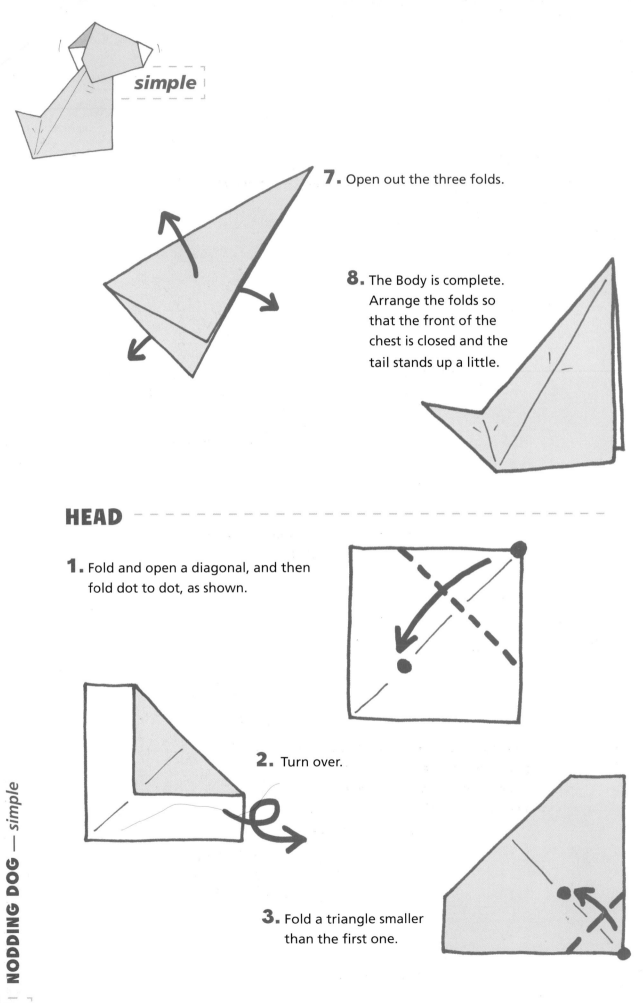

simple

7. Open out the three folds.

8. The Body is complete. Arrange the folds so that the front of the chest is closed and the tail stands up a little.

HEAD

1. Fold and open a diagonal, and then fold dot to dot, as shown.

2. Turn over.

3. Fold a triangle smaller than the first one.

4. Mountain fold the paper in half.

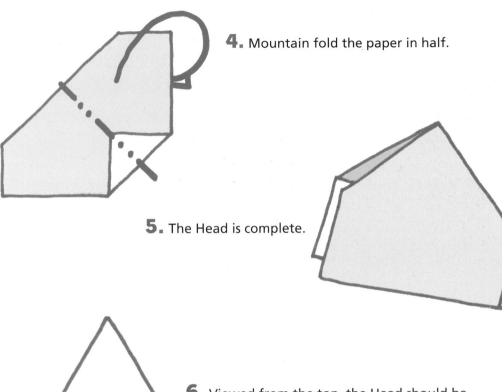

5. The Head is complete.

6. Viewed from the top, the Head should be spread open a little, like this.

ASSEMBLY

Balance the Head on the Body. Tapped lightly, the Head will nod. Alternatively, place it in an area with a light breeze and it will continually nod by itself!

PUPPET BEAK

By playing freely with the shape of the Puppet Beak's eyes and mouth, you can create many different models.

Begin with a square of origami paper, white side up.

1. By bringing two adjacent corners together, make two pinches on two adjacent edges.

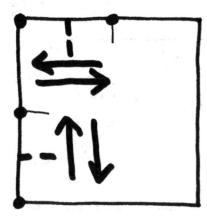

2. Now pinch two quarter creases, one above the bottom left corner and the other to the right of the top left corner.

3. Fold dot to dot, making one quarter mark touch the other, but only make a short pinch . . .

4. . . . like this. The pinch shouldn't be longer than the arrowed line. Open the paper.

5. Note the five pinches. Create and unfold the diagonal, as shown. Be careful not to crease the other diagonal by mistake!

6. Fold dot to dot as shown, beginning the fold *exactly* at the end of the sloping pinch, inside the circle.

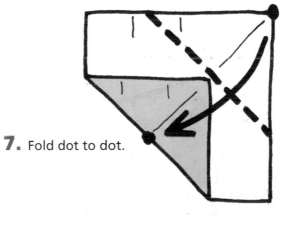

7. Fold dot to dot.

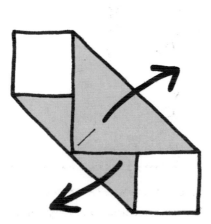

8. The paper has been divided into exact thirds! Unfold the triangles.

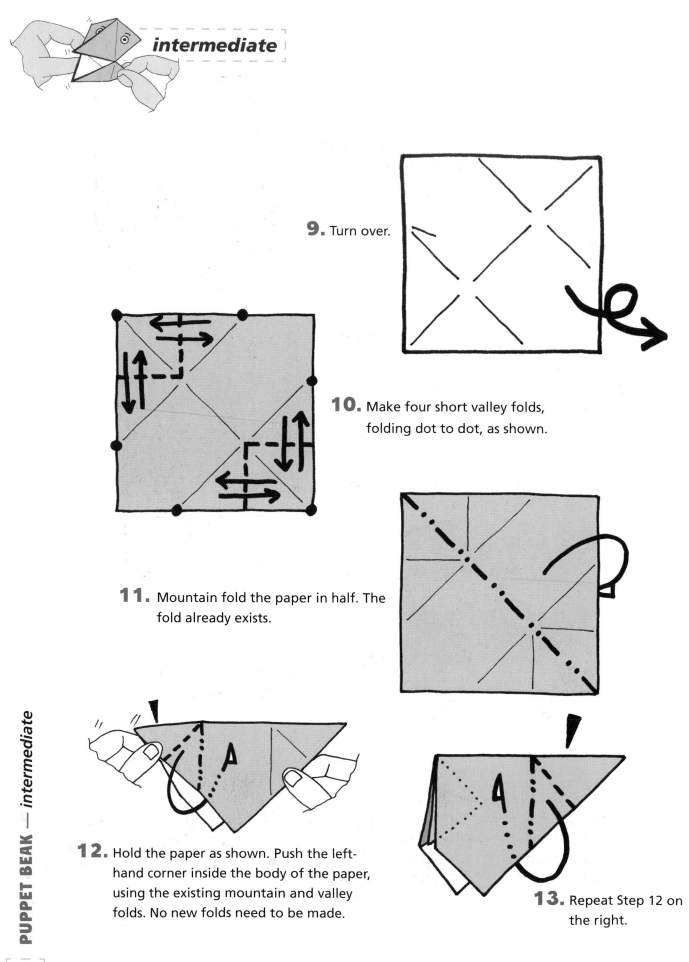

9. Turn over.

10. Make four short valley folds, folding dot to dot, as shown.

11. Mountain fold the paper in half. The fold already exists.

12. Hold the paper as shown. Push the left-hand corner inside the body of the paper, using the existing mountain and valley folds. No new folds need to be made.

13. Repeat Step 12 on the right.

14. Fold up the bottom corner. Repeat behind.

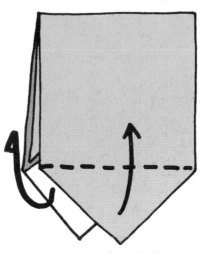

15. Fold the bottom edge up to the top edge. Repeat behind.

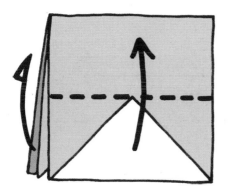

16. Front and back, valley fold the loose triangles into the center . . .

17. . . . like this. Open the paper to the final 3-D shape.

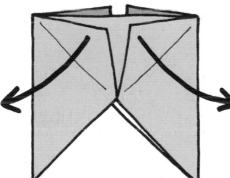

18. Draw eyes (and maybe nostrils, a tongue inside the mouth, and so on). Hold two of the triangles as shown and move your hands together and apart to make the model speak.

CROAKING FROG

I have a sneaking preference for models that are somewhat abstract, in which the subject (here, a frog) and the mechanism arise from simple geometry of the folding rather than from an overemphasis on model-making. This approach somehow creates models that are less contrived and seem to have been *discovered rather than* invented.

Begin with a square of origami paper, white side up.

1. Fold corner to corner. Unfold.

2. Similarly, fold and unfold, but between the other corners.

3. Fold the left and right corners to the center point.

4. Fold the paper in half.

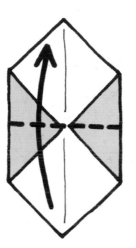

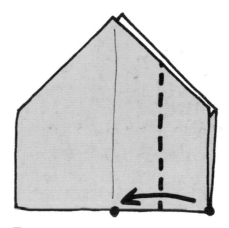

5. Fold dot to dot, bringing the right-hand edge to the center line.

6. Swing the top edge only across to the right, leaving the back edge at the center line . . .

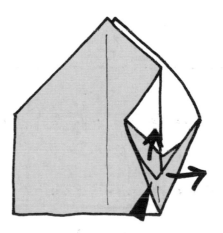

7. . . . like this. Apply pressure on the corner, so that the paper begins to flatten itself . . .

8. . . . like this. Note the combination of triangles and the color changes on the right-hand side of the paper. Repeat Steps 6–7 on the left-hand side.

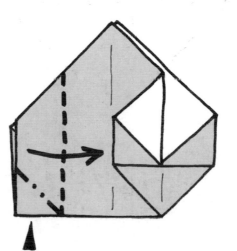

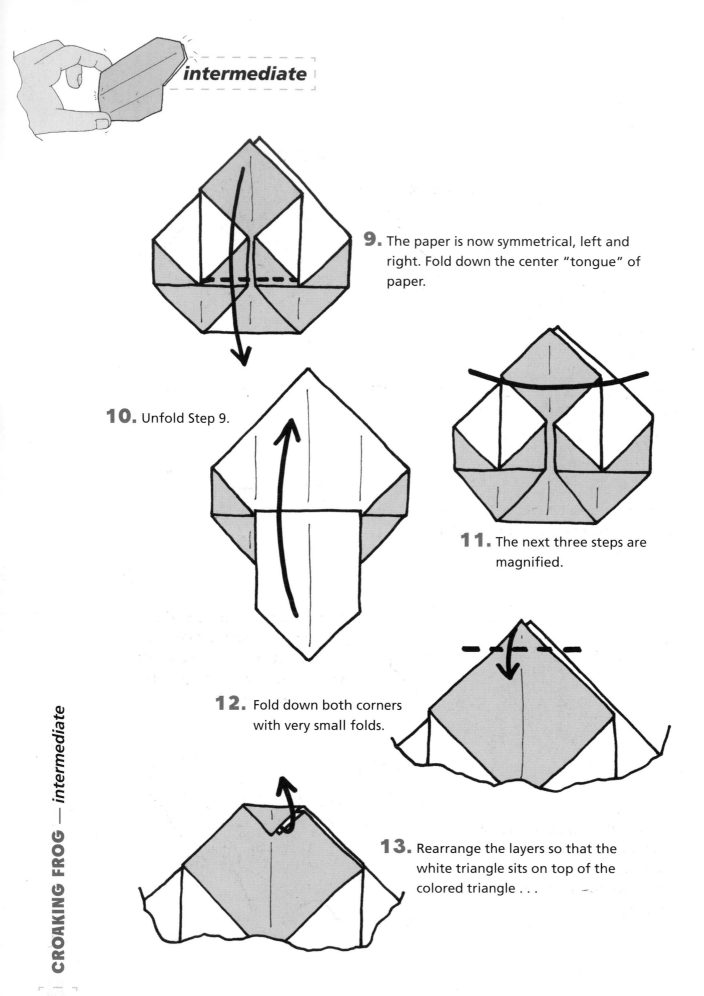

9. The paper is now symmetrical, left and right. Fold down the center "tongue" of paper.

10. Unfold Step 9.

11. The next three steps are magnified.

12. Fold down both corners with very small folds.

13. Rearrange the layers so that the white triangle sits on top of the colored triangle . . .

14. . . . like this.

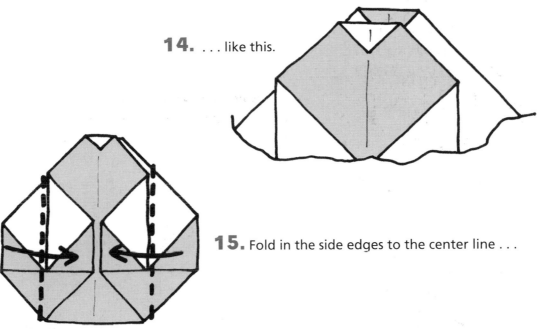

15. Fold in the side edges to the center line . . .

16. . . . and then unfold them so that seen from head-on, the paper resembles three sides of a box.

17. To make the frog croak, hold as shown on a smooth surface. Make a very short mountain fold where shown. Squeeze your finger and thumb gently together . . .

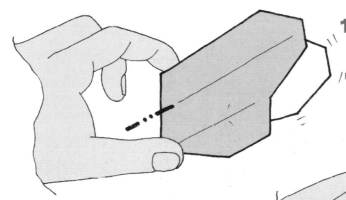

18. . . . and the jaw will snap shut. Relax your hand and the jaw will fall open under its own weight, ready for the jaw to be snapped shut again.

SCUTTLING MOUSE

The mechanism in this model is the same as in the Swimming Fish (see page 86). With extra folding, a more detailed mouse can be created, but I prefer this simple version. Use a small 4-inch (10 cm) square of paper to make a mouse-size model.

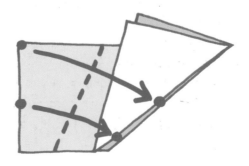

Begin with a square of origami paper, white side up.

1. Fold the top edge down to the bottom edge.

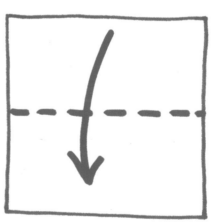

2. Fold dot to dot. This fold has a very orthodox placement, so check the shape of Step 3 to see how the paper should look. Repeat behind.

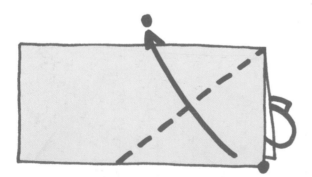

3. Fold the two dots on the left to the two dots on the right . . .

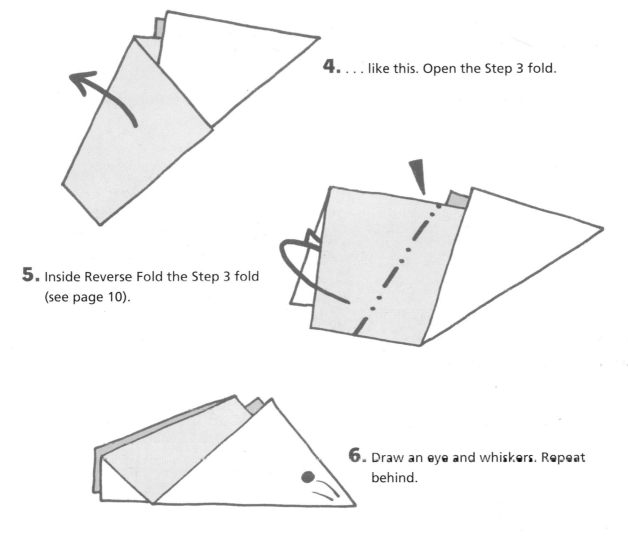

4. . . . like this. Open the Step 3 fold.

5. Inside Reverse Fold the Step 3 fold (see page 10).

6. Draw an eye and whiskers. Repeat behind.

7. To make the mouse scuttle, rub your finger and thumb together as though you are sprinkling salt. This will make the head bob from left to right. As you do this, move your hand to make the mouse look like it's moving quickly forward.

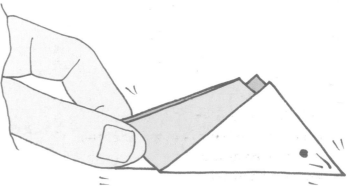

BARKING DOG 1

I've lost count of how many times this model has been published in origami magazines and books around the world . . . but usually incorrectly. The head shape is very specific but has often been mangled into something I consider unsatisfactory. Here, then, is my preferred version.

Begin with a square of origami paper, colored side up.

1. Fold corner to corner and unfold. Turn over.

2. Fold the top edges of the paper square to the center line.

3. Fold the paper in half, along the Step 1 crease.

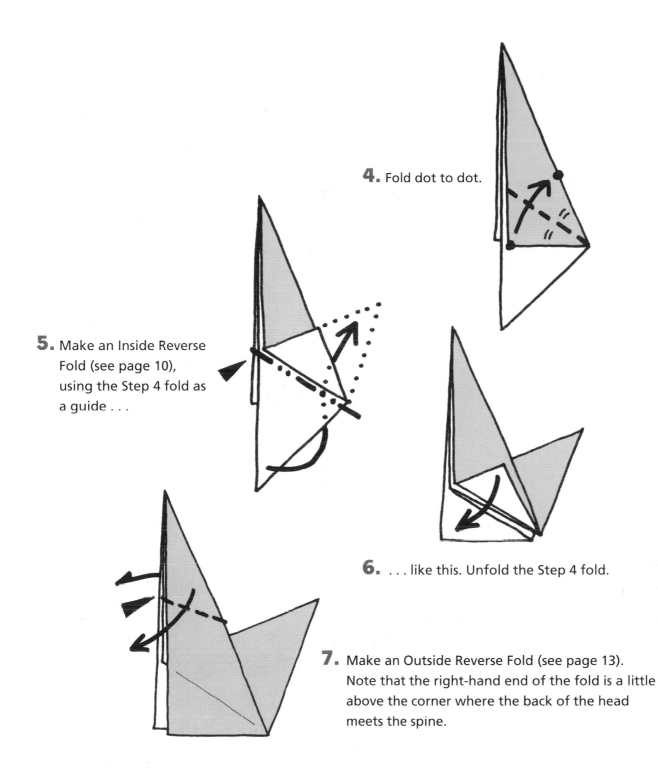

4. Fold dot to dot.

5. Make an Inside Reverse Fold (see page 10), using the Step 4 fold as a guide . . .

6. . . . like this. Unfold the Step 4 fold.

7. Make an Outside Reverse Fold (see page 13). Note that the right-hand end of the fold is a little above the corner where the back of the head meets the spine.

8. Up inside the head is a loose edge of paper. Open up the head a little to look inside and pull it all out. Press the paper flat to look like Step 9. This "growing" of the head is quite a surprising maneuver, so look carefully at Step 9 to see what you need to achieve.

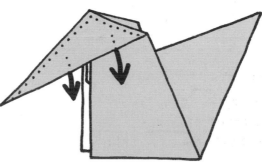

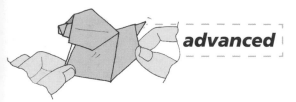

9. Make a narrow pleat to create the tail.

10. This is how the dog looks now. The remainder of the folding creates the shape of the head.

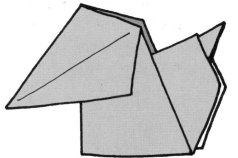

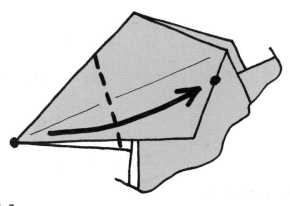

11. Fold dot to dot, exactly as shown.

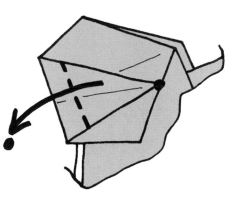

12. Again, fold dot to dot.

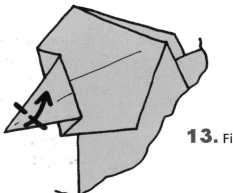

13. Finally, fold up the muzzle.

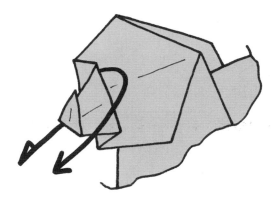

14. Unfold the previous three creases.

15. Make three Inside Reverse Folds (see page 10). Begin by making the largest, then the middle one, and then finally the smallest . . .

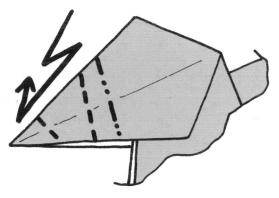

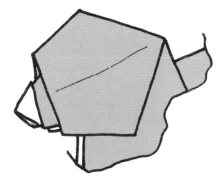

16. . . . like this.

17. The dog is complete.

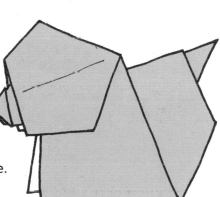

18. To make the dog bark, hold the front legs and pull the hind legs. The head will bob up and down quite realistically. Sound effects are obligatory!

BARKING DOG 2

After Barking Dog 1, I wasn't really expecting to create a different version with a different action, but somehow, from somewhere, this second version appeared by accident soon afterward. In some ways it has a better action than its better-known predecessor.

Begin with a square of origami paper, colored side up.

1. Fold corner to corner. Unfold. Turn over.

2. Fold the top edges of the paper square to the center line.

3. Fold dot to dot.

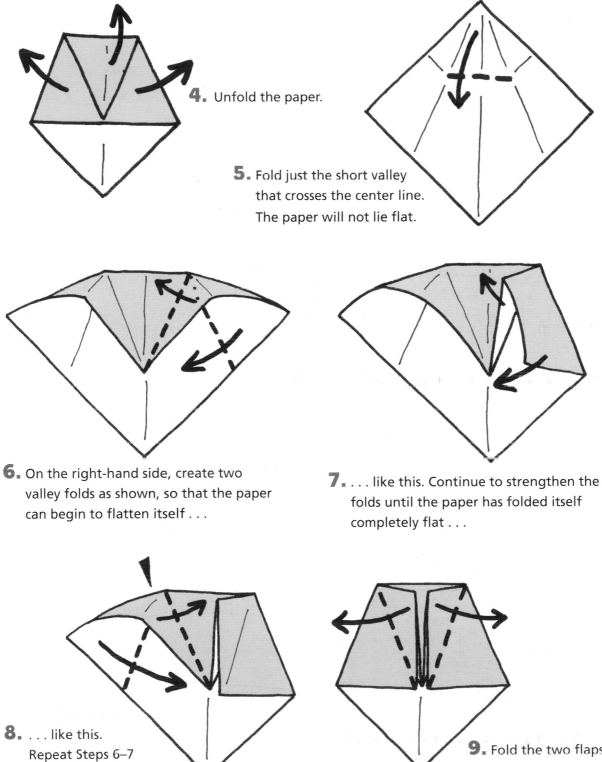

4. Unfold the paper.

5. Fold just the short valley that crosses the center line. The paper will not lie flat.

6. On the right-hand side, create two valley folds as shown, so that the paper can begin to flatten itself . . .

7. . . . like this. Continue to strengthen the folds until the paper has folded itself completely flat . . .

8. . . . like this. Repeat Steps 6–7 on the left-hand side of the paper.

9. Fold the two flaps outward, away from the center line.

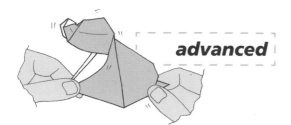

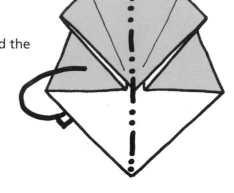

10. Mountain fold the paper in half.

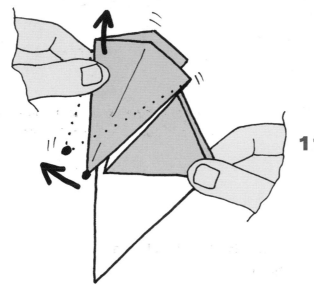

11. Hold strongly as shown. With some force, slide the paper under your left hand upward so that the new folds are made across the top of the head and at the ears, and so that the nose moves out, to the new dotted position . . .

12. . . . like this. Notice how the nose is now separated from the front legs and how extra paper has appeared at the top of the head. The only way to make the change from Step 11 to Step 12 is with brute force, so don't be too timid! Make an Inside Reverse Fold (see page 10) as shown . . .

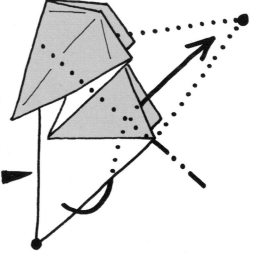

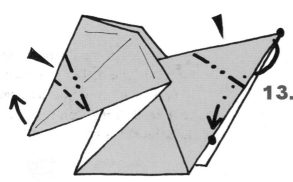

13. . . . like this. Note that the spine is not horizontal. Inside Reverse Fold the tail. Make two Inside Reverse Folds on the head . . .

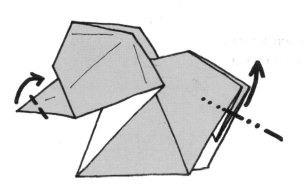

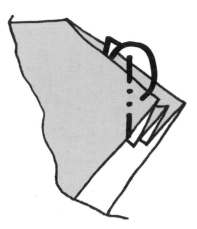

14. . . . like this. Fold the muzzle inside out. Reverse fold the tip of the tail to the position . . .

15. . . . shown here. Mountain fold the front corner inside and repeat behind . . .

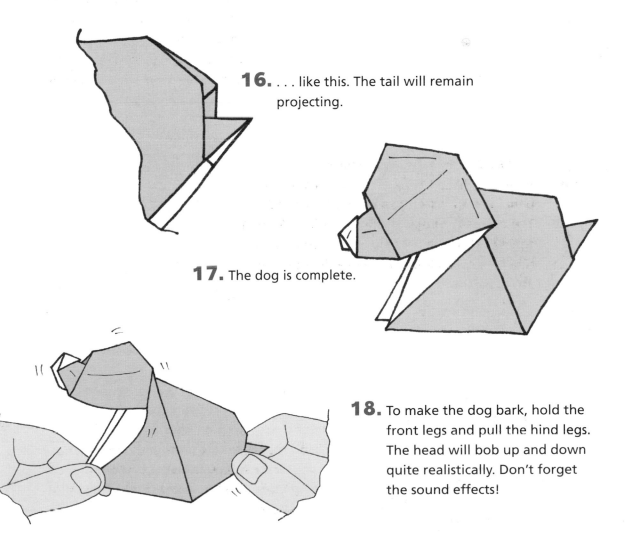

16. . . . like this. The tail will remain projecting.

17. The dog is complete.

18. To make the dog bark, hold the front legs and pull the hind legs. The head will bob up and down quite realistically. Don't forget the sound effects!

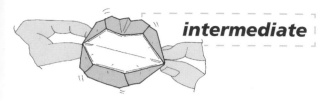

MOVING LIPS

Of all my action models, this one is probably the most literal—the lips are very representational, the action is accurate, and the color change makes the design instantly recognizable. It is also quite difficult to make well because the key folds are difficult to locate. But despite my stylistic reservations, the action is very effective . . . and that's the most important thing about an origami toy.

Begin with a square of origami paper (red for preference), color side up.

1. Fold and unfold corner to corner, but crease only where shown, a little above and to the right of the center point of the paper.

2. Fold dot to dot, but pinching only at the right-hand edge of the paper. Note how the crease would continue to the bottom left-hand corner of the square. Steps 1–2 are a minimal version of a common starting point for many models, such as Steps 1–2 of the Barking Dog 1 (see page 64).

3. Fold the top right-hand corner to the Step 2 pinch.

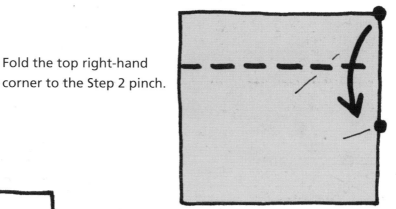

4. Unfold the paper.

5. With scissors or a knife, cut off the small rectangle.

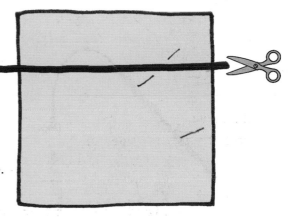

6. The larger rectangle is now in the proportion 1:√2, which is the same as European A4 paper. But since A4 paper rarely comes with two colors on the two sides, it is often necessary to make it from a square of origami paper.

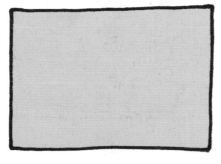

7. Turn the paper vertically and then fold in half, as shown.

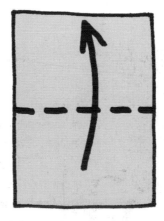

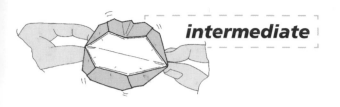

8. Fold the top layer of the paper as shown. The fold is located in the center of the paper, a little longer than a third of the width of the paper. Repeat behind.

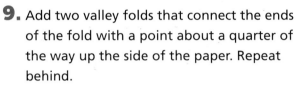

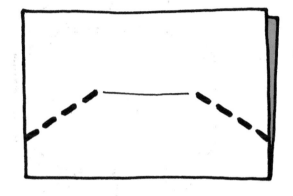

9. Add two valley folds that connect the ends of the fold with a point about a quarter of the way up the side of the paper. Repeat behind.

10. Fold dot to dot. Repeat behind.

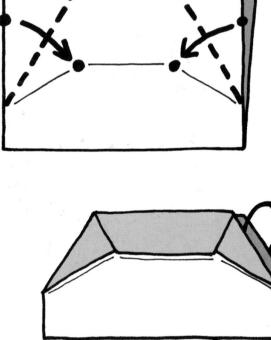

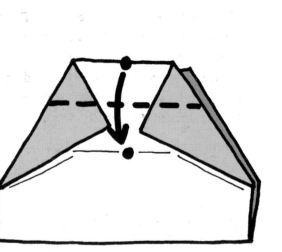

11. Again fold dot to dot. Repeat behind.

12. Unfold the center line, swinging the rear layer down from behind.

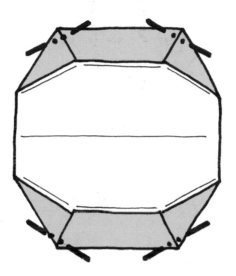

13. Round off the corners with mountain folds.

14. Make three folds on the top lip in the shape of a V.

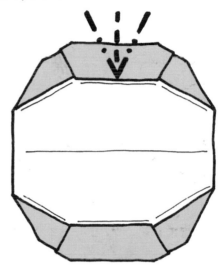

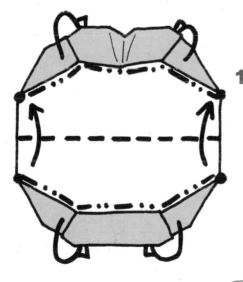

15. Shape the flat paper to become 3-D. To do this, make mountain folds around the inside edges of both lips, so that both lips can bend backward. Make a valley fold across the center of the paper. Close the mouth by folding dot to dot, left and right.

16. Hold as shown. By moving your hands gently back and forth, the lips will open and close in a surprisingly realistic manner! *Pardon, what did you say?*

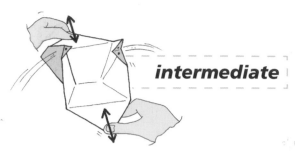

KISSING COUSINS

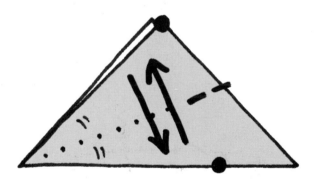

The traditional Cup in Step 7, although a model itself, is the starting point for many models. Its interesting geometry means that it can be developed in many ways, some quite complex. The folding sequence for the Kissing Cousins beyond Step 7 is unusual because only two new, small folds are made. Most of the sequence involves inverting and re-inverting the paper and refolding existing creases.

Begin with a square of origami paper, white side up.

1. Fold corner to corner.

2. Fold dot to dot, but pinch only at the right edge. If the crease were to continue, it would extend to the bottom left-hand corner.

3. Fold dot to dot.

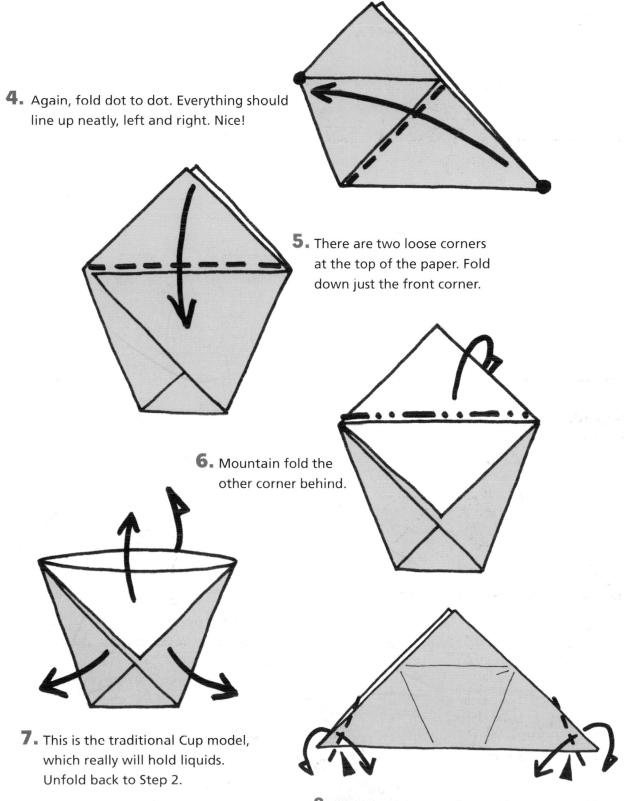

4. Again, fold dot to dot. Everything should line up neatly, left and right. Nice!

5. There are two loose corners at the top of the paper. Fold down just the front corner.

6. Mountain fold the other corner behind.

7. This is the traditional Cup model, which really will hold liquids. Unfold back to Step 2.

8. Make two very small Outside Reverse Folds (see page 13) at the bottom corners.

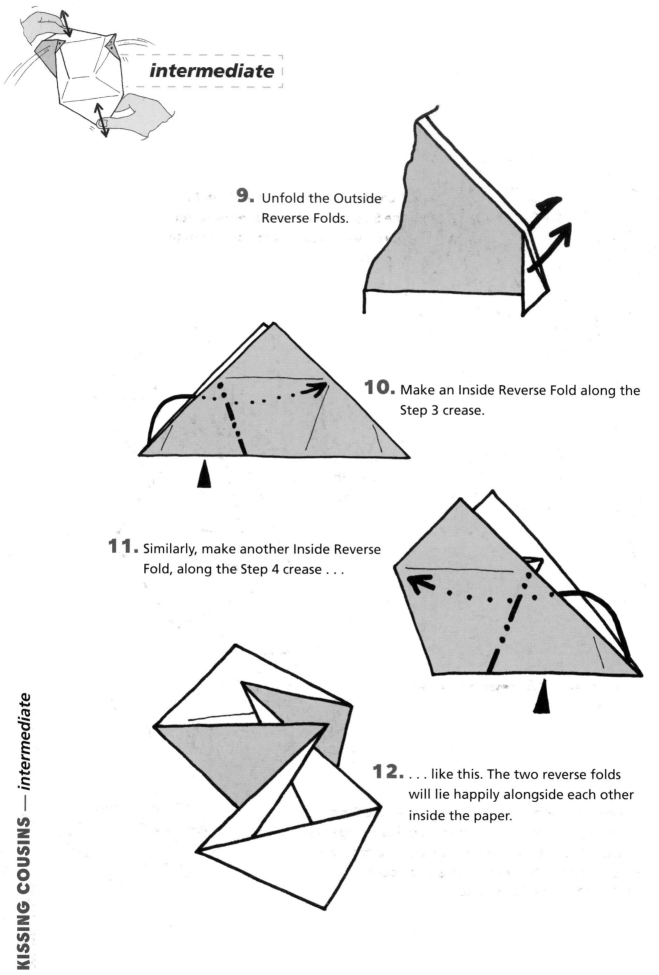

9. Unfold the Outside Reverse Folds.

10. Make an Inside Reverse Fold along the Step 3 crease.

11. Similarly, make another Inside Reverse Fold, along the Step 4 crease . . .

12. . . . like this. The two reverse folds will lie happily alongside each other inside the paper.

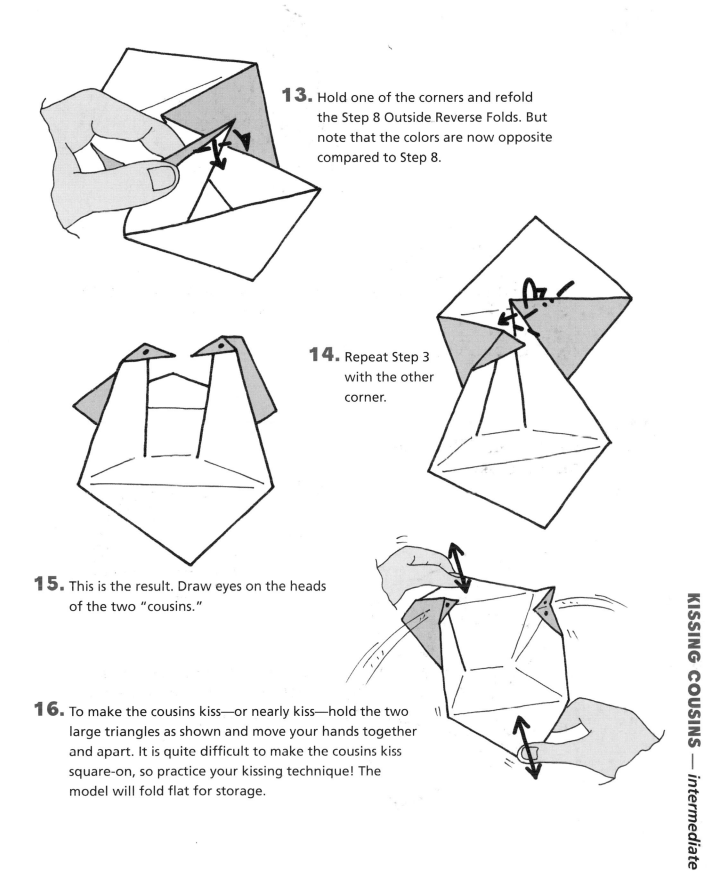

13. Hold one of the corners and refold the Step 8 Outside Reverse Folds. But note that the colors are now opposite compared to Step 8.

14. Repeat Step 3 with the other corner.

15. This is the result. Draw eyes on the heads of the two "cousins."

16. To make the cousins kiss—or nearly kiss—hold the two large triangles as shown and move your hands together and apart. It is quite difficult to make the cousins kiss square-on, so practice your kissing technique! The model will fold flat for storage.

HORSE AND RIDER

This is the most complex design in this book. Origami analyst John S. Smith has described it as unique in origami because it has two elements that move independent of each other (the horse and the rider) instead of one element moving in relation to another.

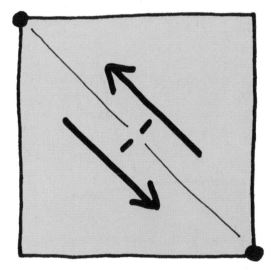

Begin with a square of origami paper, colored side up. **For best results, use paper larger than the 6-inch (15 cm) origami paper included with this book.**

1. Fold corner to corner. Unfold.

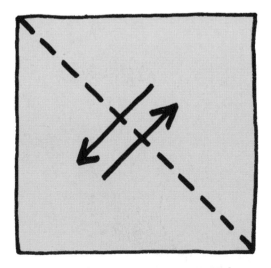

2. Fold dot to dot, pinching across the middle.

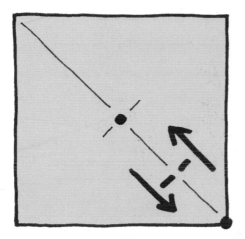

3. Fold dot to dot, pinching the quarter.

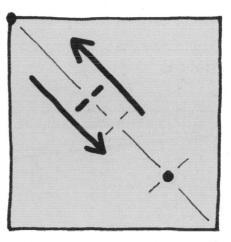

4. Fold dot to dot, pinching near the center of the paper.

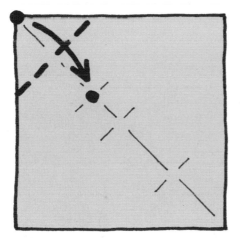

5. Now fold the corner to the pinch just made.

6. Unfold the Step 5 crease. Turn the paper over.

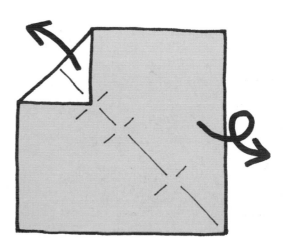

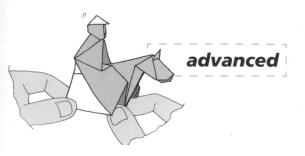

advanced

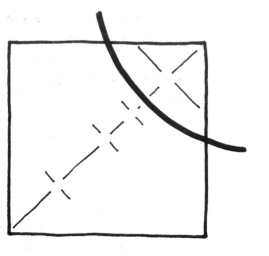

7. This is the pattern of folds and pinches. Step 8 is a magnification of the corner.

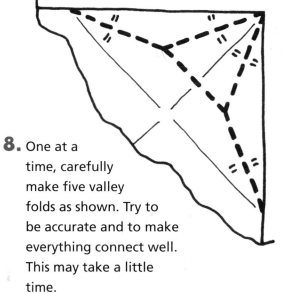

8. One at a time, carefully make five valley folds as shown. Try to be accurate and to make everything connect well. This may take a little time.

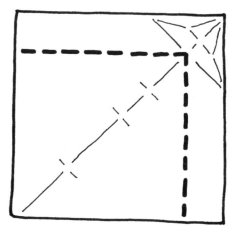

9. Make two valley folds, as shown.

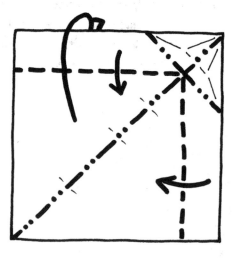

10. The paper will now collapse obligingly to make Step 11. Make the four mountains and two valleys simultaneously. Make sure to check with Step 11 to see what you are trying to achieve.

11. Valley fold the white triangle as shown, but where the paper is colored, make an Inside Reverse Fold (see page 10) . . .

12. . . . like this. Check carefully how the paper is layered and colored. Repeat Step 11 behind. Make an Inside Reverse Fold, as shown. Look ahead to Step 13 to see the result. Try to be exact.

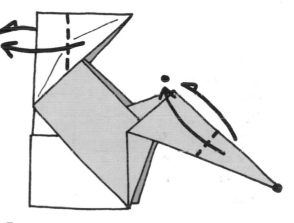

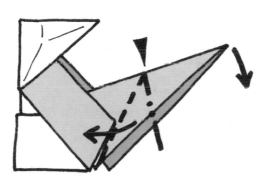

13. Make two reverse folds as shown—a long valley and a shorter mountain. This will lower the head. Again, try to be exact.

14. Fold the tip of the horse's head backward to a point just a little beyond the back of the head. Fold the white triangle along the fold made in Step 8.

15. Narrow the front leg with a long valley fold, which will then allow you to narrow the horse's head by folding the bottom edge inside. Repeat behind. Fold the ear forward, flat against the top of the head.

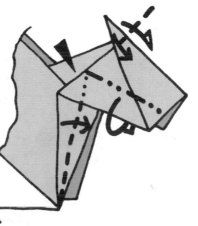

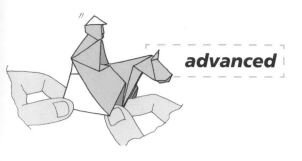

16. Shape the muzzle. Repeat behind.

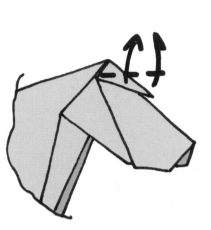

17. Reverse fold the ear so that it sticks up into the air. This is a very small fold, and it may be difficult to make it perfectly.

18. The horse's head is complete.

19. Refold the long valley fold across the white triangle, pushing in the paper inside to make a new horizontal mountain fold where shown . . .

20. . . . like this. Repeat behind. Create a nose by making two reverse folds. Create a cap by turning the corner of the paper inside out. Allow the peak of the cap to protrude out over the top of the nose . . .

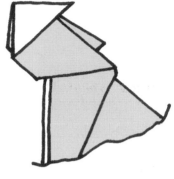

21. . . . like this. If your head looks a little different, adjust the folds.

22. Pull out the "leg" of the rider from inside the horse's front leg. Repeat behind. Make a mountain and valley fold as shown to create the arms and hands of the rider. Repeat behind.

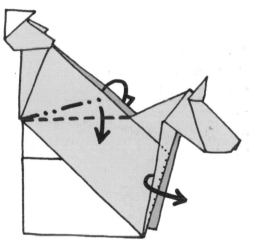

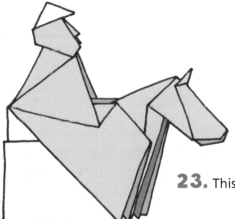

23. This is the final result. Well done!

24. To make the horse and rider both move, hold the white corner in one hand and the horse's front legs in the other (note how the rider's "feet" cover your thumb and finger). Move your right hand up gently and down to make the horse's head bob up and down. At the same time, move your left hand to make the rider also bob up and down. With a little practice and coordination between the hands, the action of the two movements relative to one another is very effective.

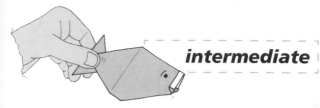

SWIMMING FISH

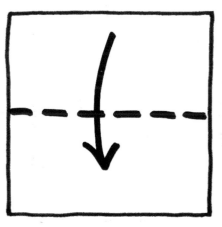

The rubbing action to make this fish swim is one I borrowed from a design I saw in a Japanese book or magazine (which, despite my best efforts, I have been unable to trace) but folded very differently. I remember thinking at the time that the mechanism was a wonderful idea, so I redesigned the fish as the version you see here. The same action is used in the Scuttling Mouse.

Use a square of origami paper, white side up.

1. Fold the top edge down to the bottom edge.

2. Fold and unfold across the middle.

3. Mountain fold the corner inside the paper. Repeat behind.

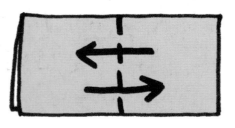

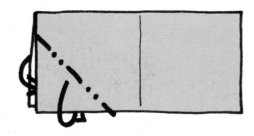

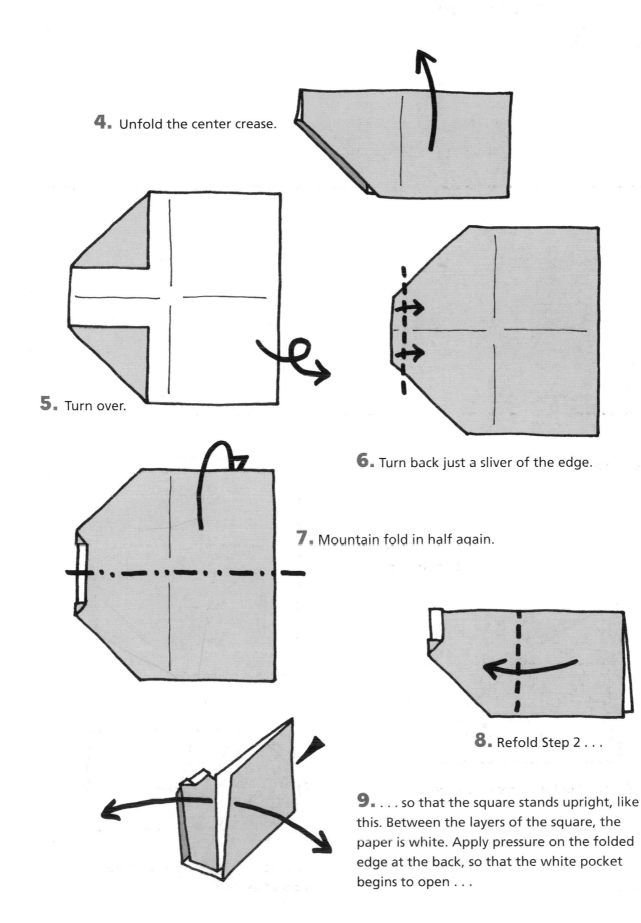

4. Unfold the center crease.

5. Turn over.

6. Turn back just a sliver of the edge.

7. Mountain fold in half again.

8. Refold Step 2 . . .

9. . . . so that the square stands upright, like this. Between the layers of the square, the paper is white. Apply pressure on the folded edge at the back, so that the white pocket begins to open . . .

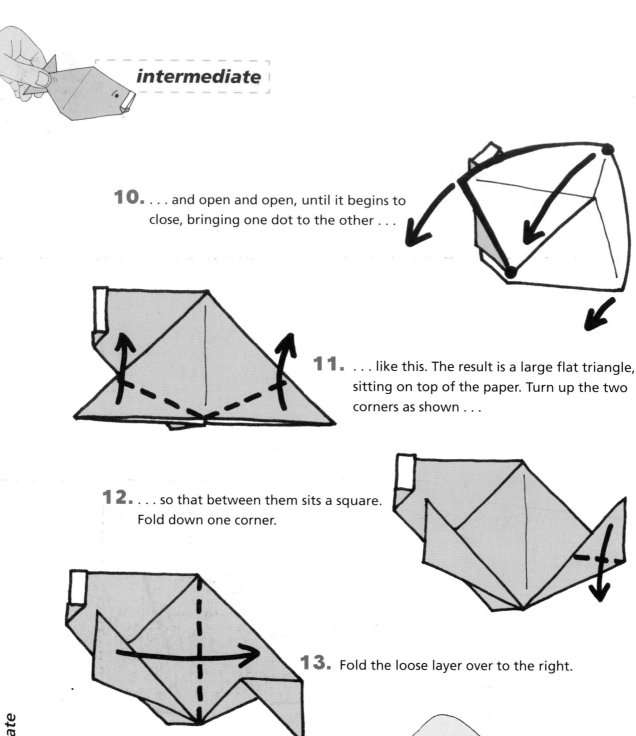

10. . . . and open and open, until it begins to close, bringing one dot to the other . . .

11. . . . like this. The result is a large flat triangle, sitting on top of the paper. Turn up the two corners as shown . . .

12. . . . so that between them sits a square. Fold down one corner.

13. Fold the loose layer over to the right.

14. This is the completed fish. Add an eye.

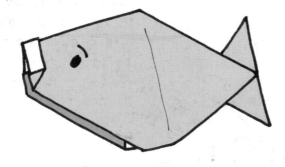

15. To make the fish swim, hold as shown. Rub your finger and thumb together as though sprinkling salt. This will cause the fish to swim left and right! To complete the effect, move your hand forward at the same time.

BIG BEAK

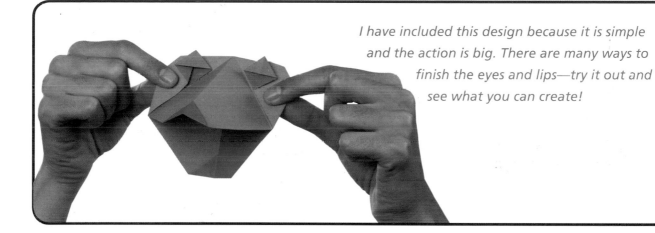

I have included this design because it is simple and the action is big. There are many ways to finish the eyes and lips—try it out and see what you can create!

Begin with a square of origami paper, colored side up.

1. Fold an edge to the opposite edge. Unfold.

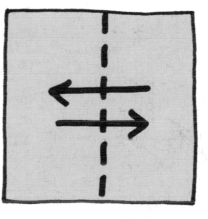

2. Similarly, fold an adjacent edge to the opposite side. Unfold.

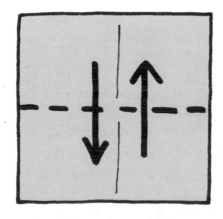

3. There are now two long valley folds crossing the paper. If, by some chance, one of them is a mountain, Step 13 will not open and the model will not work. Turn the paper over.

4. Fold and unfold a diagonal.

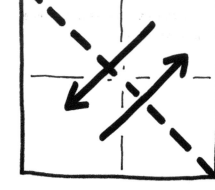

6. Fold dot to dot, bringing the corners to the center point.

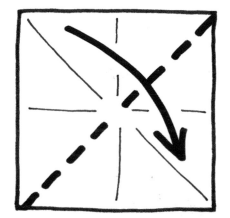

5. Fold the other diagonal.

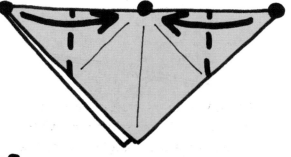

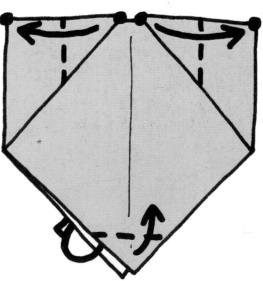

7. At the top, fold dot to dot. At the bottom, fold up the front corner a little, then repeat behind with the rear corner . . .

8. . . . like this. The next step is a magnification.

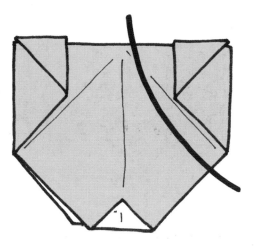

9. Stand the small triangle upright.

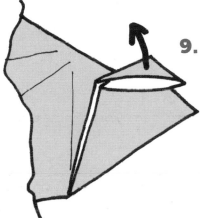

10. Apply pressure on the back edge of the triangle. This will open the white pocket inside the triangle. Squash the pocket flat, folding dot to dot . . .

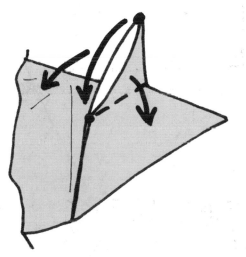

11. . . . like this. Repeat with the other eye.

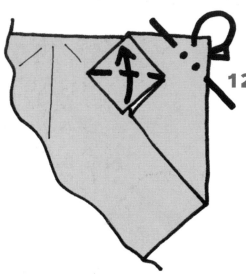

12. Mountain fold the corner behind. On the eye, fold the loose corner up to the top, exposing the white square beneath. Repeat with the other eye.

13. The folding is now complete. To give the model its 3-D shape, make two valleys and a mountain as shown. The same folds are made on the back, opening the beak. Together, these are the folds made in Steps 1–5.

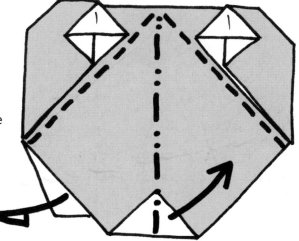

14. To make the model work, hold as shown at the sides of the mouth. Move your hands gently back and forth and the mouth will open and close with large movements!

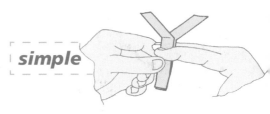

PAPER ORCHESTRA

I'm fascinated with the acoustic properties of paper—how sounds can be made with paper by tearing, tapping, blowing, vibrating, wobbling, scrunching, and so on. Some of these sounds don't require any origami techniques, but some of them do. What follows is a selection of some of these

origami-based instruments, particularly percussive ones. There are many others. If you want to hear paper music and read suggestions on how you can make your own live or recorded performances, please visit www.papersonics.com.

CLACKER

As a child, I used to make this from a flattened paper straw. But since paper straws are now hard to find, I created this origami alternative.

Begin with a sheet of regular 8½ x 11-inch copy paper or European A4 paper.

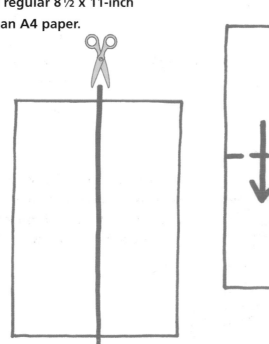

1. Cut the paper in half.

2. Fold in half across the middle. Unfold.

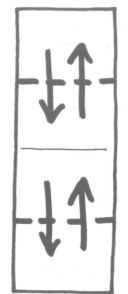

3. Fold the top and bottom edges to the center fold. Unfold.

4. Fold in half down the center. Unfold.

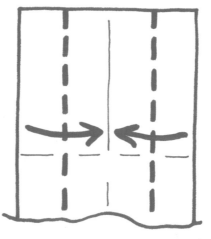

5. Fold the long edges to the center line.

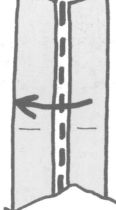

6. Fold in half along the Step 4 crease.

7. Fold in half along the Step 2 crease.

8. Fold the Step 3 creases.

9. This is the completed model.

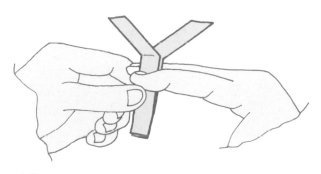

10. To make a loud *clack!*, hold tightly as shown. Note that the paper is not shaped like a T, but like a Y. A little experimentation will show you the best angle for the loudest sound. Grip the stem of the Y lightly between your first and second fingers and whip them upward as fast as you can . . .

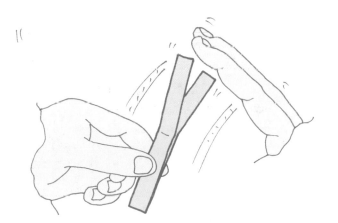

11. . . . like this. The faster you can move your hand, the louder will be the sound. Sometimes the very loudest sounds are made when the fingers do not touch the stem at all.

LIP SMACKER

The mechanism shown here is a simplification of the one used to make the Snapping Crocodile 2 (see page 44). You can create surprisingly intricate rhythms by holding a Lip Smacker in each hand and playing in concert with other people.

Begin with a sheet of 8½ x 11-inch card stock or European A4 card stock (not regular paper).

Try making the Lip Smacker in different sizes for different pitches of sound.

1. Bring the top corners together and make a small pinch at the top edge.

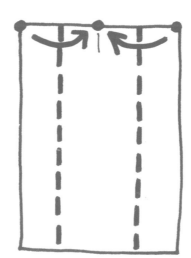

2. Fold the top corners to the center pinch.

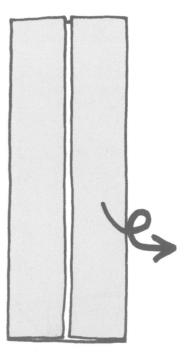

3. Turn over.

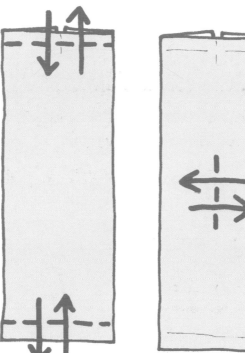

4. Fold and unfold narrow rectangles at the top and bottom edges.

5. Fold and unfold a valley fold in the center as shown. Don't make it too lengthy, and try to position it centrally between the top and bottom edges . . .

6. . . . like this. Turn over.

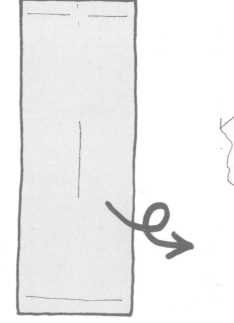

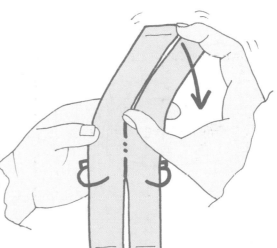

7. Hold as shown, with your thumb against the top end of the Step 5 crease. Gently squeeze the sides of the paper with your left hand while pulling down the top edge with your right hand . . .

simple

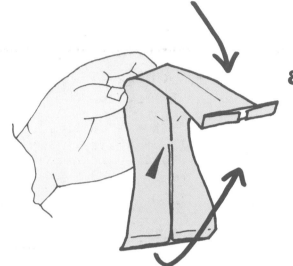

8. . . . like this. The result looks very much like Step 20 of the Snapping Crocodile 2. Turn the card upside down and repeat the Step 7 procedure with the other end of the paper . . .

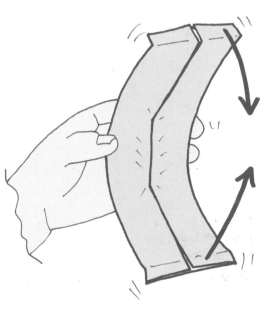

9. . . . like this. Note that the Step 5 crease has formed, enabling the top and bottom edges to *smack!* loudly together . . .

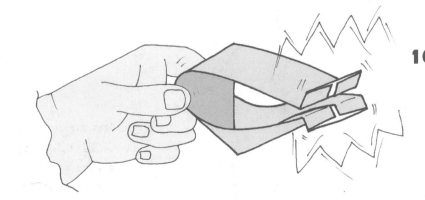

10. . . . like this. Move your finger and thumb around a little so that the "lips" will move around a bit relative to each other and slap neatly together.

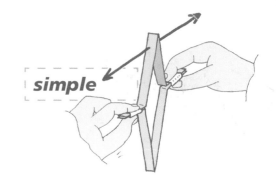

WHIP CRACK

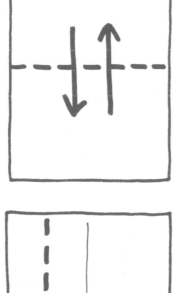

Made well, this is the loudest of all origami-based percussive instruments. It can be made any size—even very, very big!—but for starters, I recommend a sheet of regular 8½ x 11-inch copy paper or European A4 paper.

1. Fold the paper across the middle. Unfold.

2. Fold the paper down the middle. Unfold.

3. Fold the left edge to the center fold. Unfold.

4. Cut down the center line and the quarter line . . .

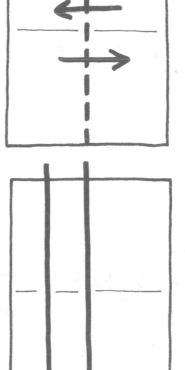

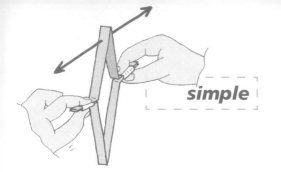

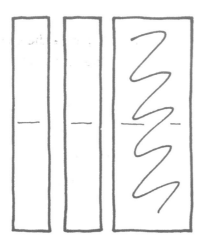

5. . . . like this. Keep the two narrow pieces and discard the large piece on the right (or perhaps make another Whip Crack with it!).

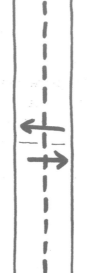

6. Fold in half. Unfold.

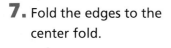

7. Fold the edges to the center fold.

8. Fold in half along the Step 6 crease.

9. Repeat Steps 6–8 with the other piece of paper.

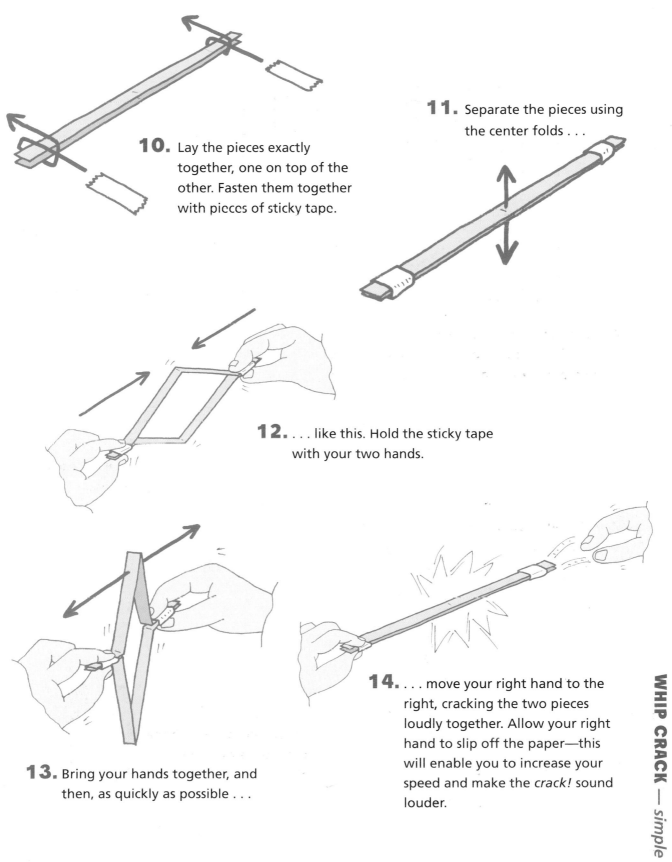

10. Lay the pieces exactly together, one on top of the other. Fasten them together with pieces of sticky tape.

11. Separate the pieces using the center folds . . .

12. . . . like this. Hold the sticky tape with your two hands.

13. Bring your hands together, and then, as quickly as possible . . .

14. . . . move your right hand to the right, cracking the two pieces loudly together. Allow your right hand to slip off the paper—this will enable you to increase your speed and make the *crack!* sound louder.

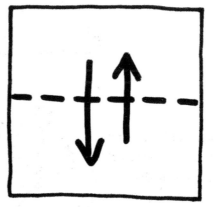

WORLD'S BEST DREIDL

I used to teach a day a week at a particular college and would habitually arrive early to organize my materials. One day I finished my preparation unusually early, and to occupy myself, I started to fold. Without any unfolding or refolding, I straightaway folded the design here, recognizing it as a dreidl. A discarded smoker's match fitted snugly inside, and voilà . . . I had created what I consider to be one of my best designs.

Begin with a square of origami paper, white side up.

1. Fold across the middle. Unfold.

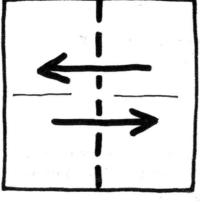

2. Fold down the middle. Unfold.

3. Fold the four corners to the center point.

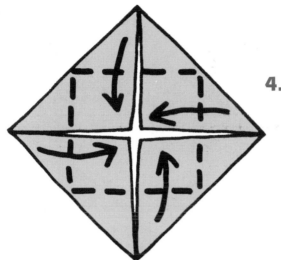

4. Again, fold the four corners to the center point.

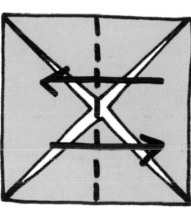

5. Fold down the middle. Unfold.

6. Fold the bottom edge up to the top.

7. Hold as shown. Move your hands upward and toward each other, so that the pocket at the top begins to open . . .

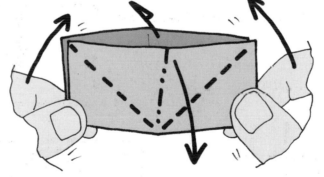

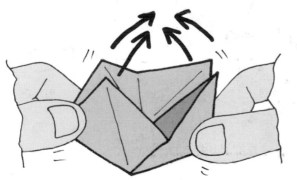

8. . . . like this. Continue to bring your hands together until the pocket closes up again . . .

9. . . . like this. Notice there are four triangles that meet at the center. Flatten the paper so there are two triangles on the left and two on the right.

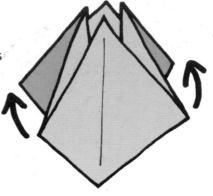

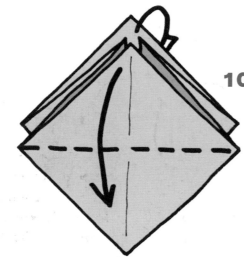

10. Fold down only the front corner. Turn over and repeat behind.

11. The paper now resembles a sailboat. Fold the left and right front corners to the center point. Turn over and repeat behind.

13. . . . like this. Notice how the paper is now thick at the right and thin at the left. Turn over.

12. Fold the front corner at the left across to the right . . .

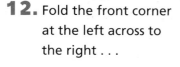

14. Fold the front layer at the left across to the right. The paper will become symmetrical again.

15. Fold the front corner at the top down to the bottom corner. Turn over and repeat behind.

16. Fan out the four arms in the shape of a cross . . .

17. . . . like this. Insert a wooden match into the hole at the top and push it all the way to the bottom. It should grip well.

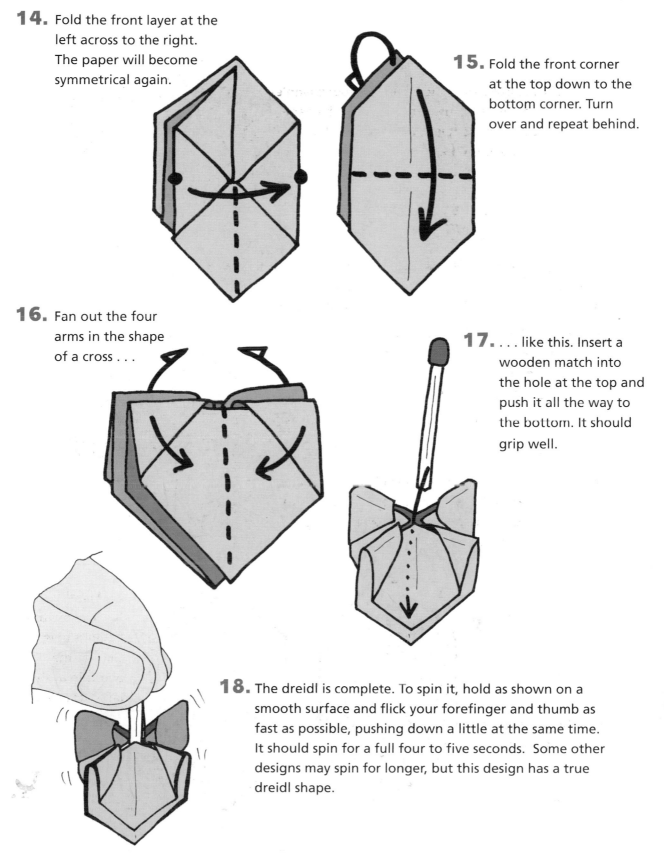

18. The dreidl is complete. To spin it, hold as shown on a smooth surface and flick your forefinger and thumb as fast as possible, pushing down a little at the same time. It should spin for a full four to five seconds. Some other designs may spin for longer, but this design has a true dreidl shape.

DOMINO RALLY

One of the all-time classics of origami is the Koton Kon (in Japanese), or Ta-rum-te-rum-tum (in English), a folded tumbler designed by Seiryo Takakawa (Japan). Placed precisely apart, each tumbler will roll over and knock over the next in line, much like a domino rally. However, in my opinion, these original tumblers lack the momentum to knock into the next with enough force to guarantee it will fall over. So I designed this version of the Takakawa classic with extra weight at the top for more clout.

Begin with a sheet of regular 8½ x 11-inch copy paper or European A4 paper.

1. Fold up the bottom edge to lie against the left edge.

2. Fold the top rectangle over the triangle.

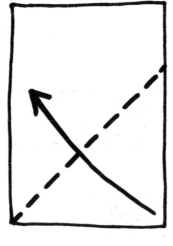

3. Keep the rectangle folded over, but unfold the triangle . . .

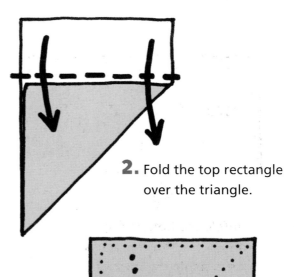

4. . . . like this. Fold in half down the middle. Unfold.

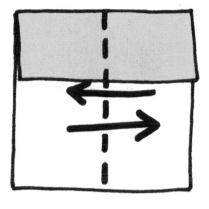

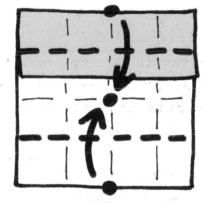

5. Fold in half across the middle. Unfold.

6. Fold the left and right edges to the center line. Unfold.

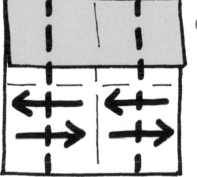

7. Fold the top and bottom edges to the center line.

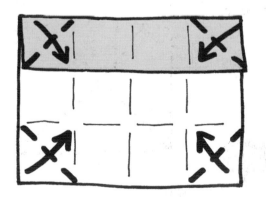

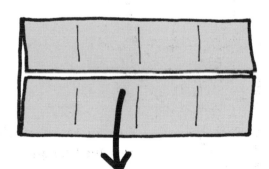

8. Unfold the bottom flap only. Note how this flap is just a single thickness of paper. The unfolded flap is quite thick.

9. Fold in the corners, as shown.

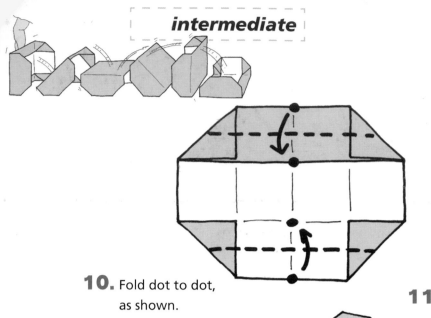

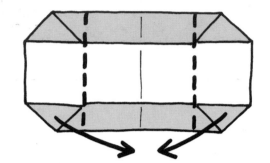

10. Fold dot to dot, as shown.

11. Note how the paper looks the same at the top and bottom, but the top edge is much thicker than the bottom edge. Fold in the sides along the existing creases. Flatten the paper as though closing the doors of a cupboard, and then open them halfway to look like Step 12.

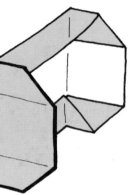

12. This is the completed model. Make sure that the sides stand away at exactly 90 degrees to the back.

13. Stand the model on a level surface, with the thick edge at the top. With just a gentle nudge, knock it over. Under its own momentum, the model will tumble through 3/4 of a circle to eventually lie on its back! With the thin edge at the top, it will not tumble.

14. You are now ready to make the Domino Rally, in which each "domino" will tumble and knock over the next one. The critical factor for success is to space the dominos an exact distance apart. This is easily done by taking a sheet of the 8½ x 11-inch or A4 paper you made the dominoes with and using it to separate the dominoes by the length of the short edge, as shown. You should arrange the dominoes with some precision, spacing them carefully. After making the chain, you can try to create a pyramid effect, in which one domino tumbles to knock over a pair placed side by side, which in turn tumble to turn knock over two pairs, which in turn tumble to knock over four pairs, and so on!

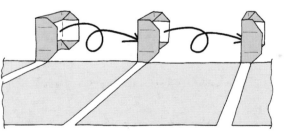

PENCIL PROPELLER

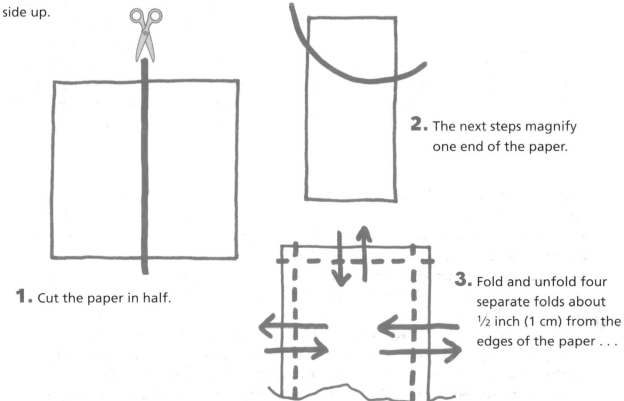

One of my happiest origami memories is from an origami convention in which someone showed me how to make a propeller that would spin around on the end of your finger when you walked briskly forward. We spent a very silly couple of hours devising ever-more ridiculous obstacle courses to negotiate. This is my larger, more high-tech version of a great toy.

Begin with a square of origami paper, white side up.

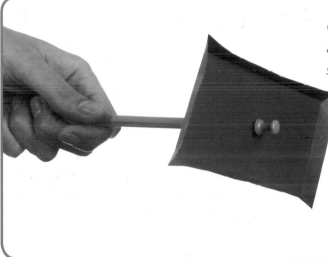

1. Cut the paper in half.

2. The next steps magnify one end of the paper.

3. Fold and unfold four separate folds about ½ inch (1 cm) from the edges of the paper . . .

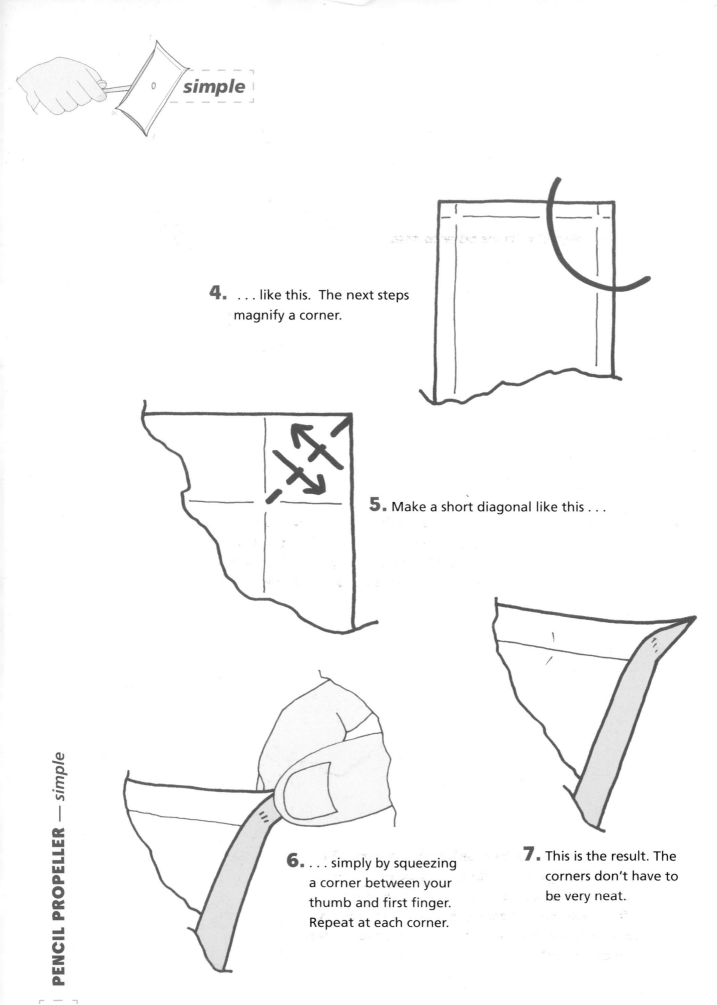

simple

4. . . . like this. The next steps magnify a corner.

5. Make a short diagonal like this . . .

6. . . . simply by squeezing a corner between your thumb and first finger. Repeat at each corner.

7. This is the result. The corners don't have to be very neat.

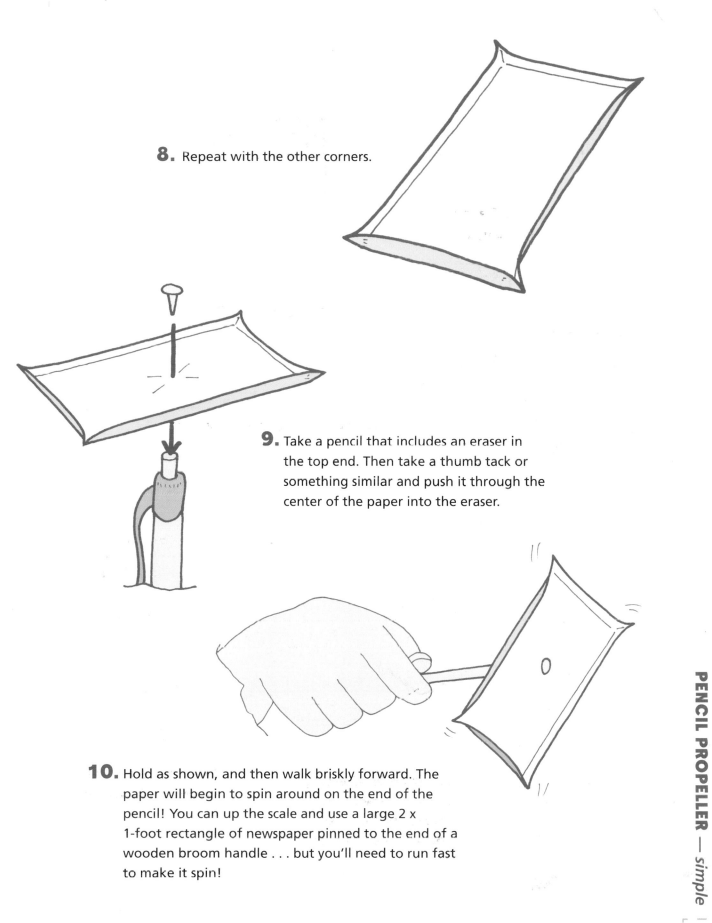

8. Repeat with the other corners.

9. Take a pencil that includes an eraser in the top end. Then take a thumb tack or something similar and push it through the center of the paper into the eraser.

10. Hold as shown, and then walk briskly forward. The paper will begin to spin around on the end of the pencil! You can up the scale and use a large 2 x 1-foot rectangle of newspaper pinned to the end of a wooden broom handle . . . but you'll need to run fast to make it spin!

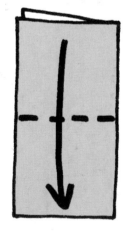

QUASAR

Modular action models are unusual—
"modular" meaning models assembled from
identical units. This one makes a dramatic
spinning silhouette, but if you have trouble
focusing on it right in front of your face, try
blowing on it in front of a mirror and looking
at the reflection.

Take two squares of origami paper, and cut them so that they are
roughly 4½ inches (12 cm) square each. Place white side up.

1. Fold the right edge across to the left
edge.

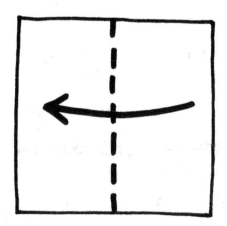

2. Fold the top edge down to the bottom
edge.

3. Check that you have four corners at the bottom left, and then fold just the top corner of the four up to the top right corner . . .

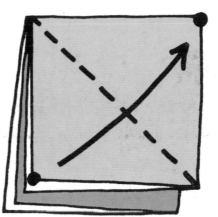

4. . . . like this. Turn over.

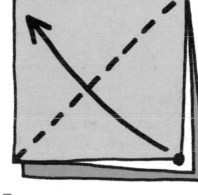

5. There are now three corners at the bottom right. Fold just the top corner of the three up to the top left corner . . .

6. . . . like this.

7. Repeat Steps 1–6 to make a second module. Place them in front of you as shown, with three corners at the top left, and then rotate the right-hand module through 180 degrees . . .

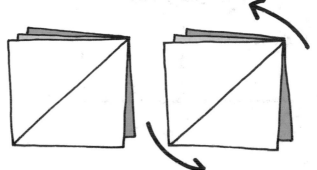

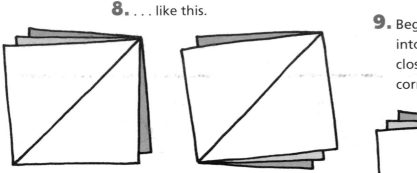

8. . . . like this.

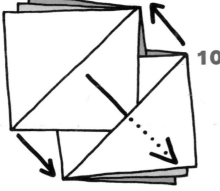

9. Begin to interleaf one module into the other, as shown. Look closely at the layering of the corners as they interleaf.

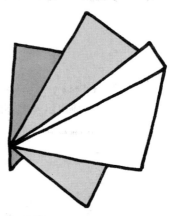

10. Continue to push the modules together, putting the corner of the top module under the sloping edge of the bottom module, as shown. Repeat behind.

11. Push the modules completely together, leaving three corners at the top left and bottom right corners. Fan out the thin corners at the top and bottom . . .

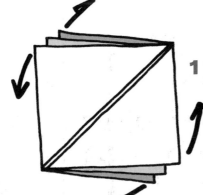

12. . . . like this.

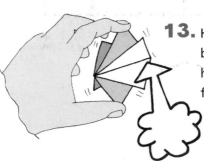

13. Hold the thick corners at the top and bottom of the model between your first finger and thumb. Blow onto the right-hand edge of the Quasar and it will begin to spin around very fast. Don't blow onto the middle because that will not make it spin—you must blow onto the edge. The Quasar will make a beautiful spinning pattern of color and white.

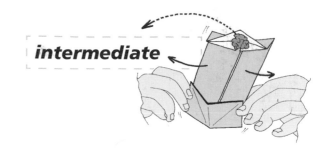

CATAPULT

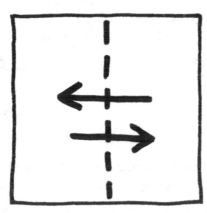

Many handheld origami toys involve one element moving back and forth against a static element—the head of the Barking Dog 1 against the body, the upper jaw of Snapping Crocodile 1 against the bottom jaw, and so on. If these gentle movements are exaggerated, and a lever is made long enough, a catapult design becomes possible. With practice, the catapult shown here will shoot a projectile more than 17 feet.

Use an 8-inch (20 cm) square of strong paper.

1. Fold in half down the middle. Unfold.

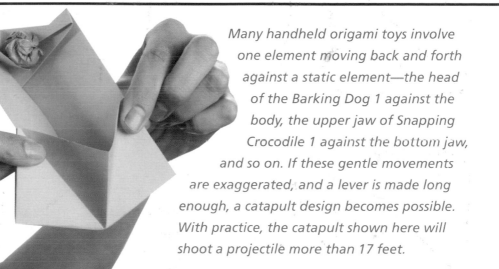

2. Fold the edges to the center line. Unfold.

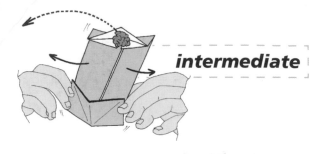

3. Fold in the bottom corners, as shown.

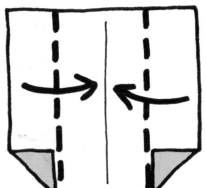

4. Refold the Step 2 creases.

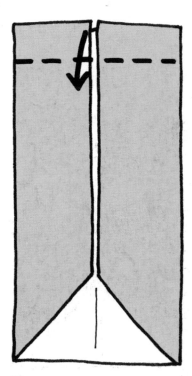

5. Fold down just a little of the top edge.

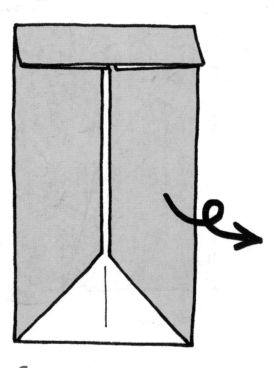

6. Turn over.

7. Fold the bottom edge across to lie on the right-hand edge. Unfold.

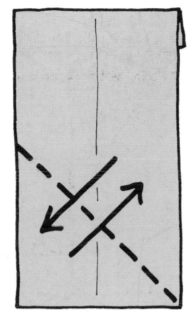

8. Similarly, fold the bottom edge to lie against the left-hand edge. Unfold.

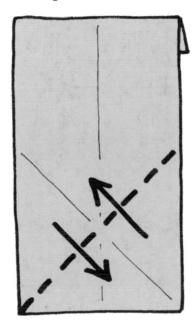

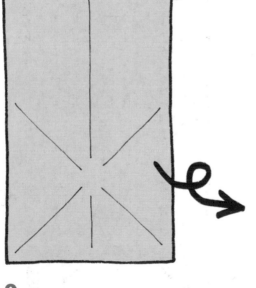

9. Turn over.

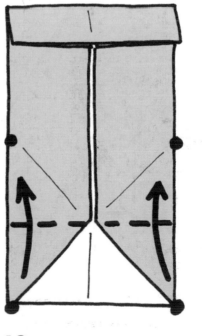

10. Fold dot to dot, as shown.

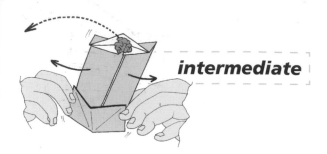

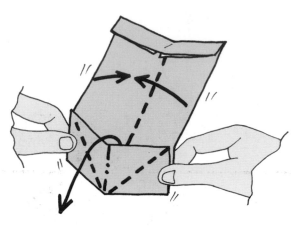

11. Hold as shown. Gently bring your hands together, allowing the paper to fold in half and the V edge near the bottom to swing downward . . .

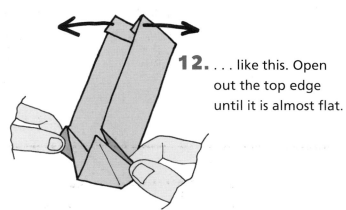

12. . . . like this. Open out the top edge until it is almost flat.

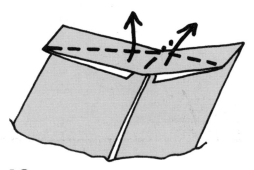

13. On the top layer only, make two valley folds in the shape of an upturned V . . .

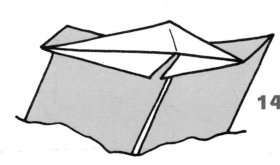

14. . . . like this. This will open a white pocket in the paper.

15. Crumple up a tight ball of paper and put it in the white pocket created in Steps 13–14. To make the Catapult work, hold tightly as shown, at the top of the V of valley folds. Swing your hands quickly apart and the ball will launch into the air! The paper will sometimes rip at the bottom of the V. To prevent this, and to launch the paper ball with more vigor, reinforce the edge at the bottom of the V with sticky tape.

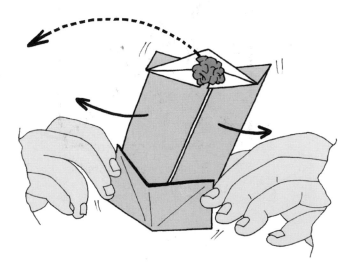

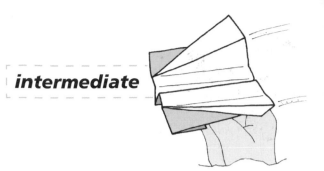

THE CUTTER

I love paper planes! The process of folding a design that is pleasing to make, followed by the innocent delight as it flies beautifully through the air (hopefully!), is a magical feeling difficult to describe and which I wish to repeat again and again. This design is an unusually fast flier, cutting recklessly through the air.

Use a square of origami paper, white side up.

1. Begin with Step 6 of the Puppet Beak (see page 55).

2. Fold the other diagonal. Unfold.

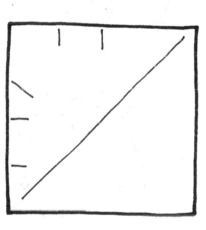

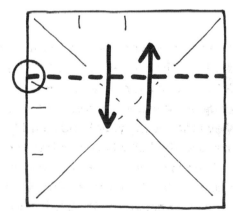

3. Using the circled location crease as a guide, make a horizontal fold. Unfold.

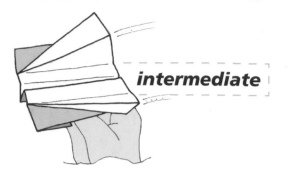

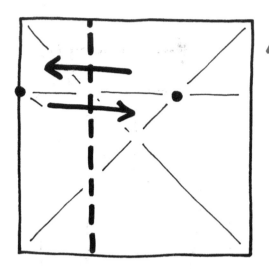

4. Fold dot to dot. Unfold.

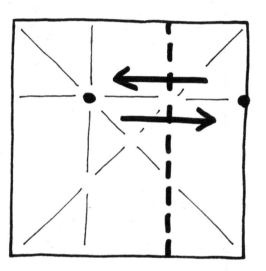

5. Fold dot to dot. Unfold.

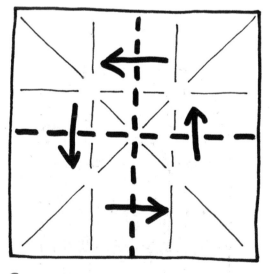

6. Fold the horizontal and vertical center lines. Unfold.

7. Fold dot to dot. Unfold.

8. Fold dot to dot. Do not unfold.

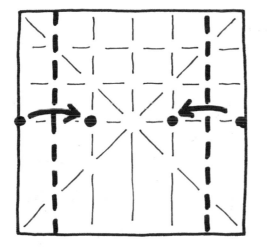

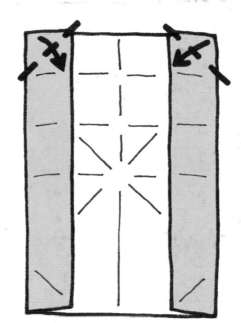

9. At the top, fold in the colored corners.

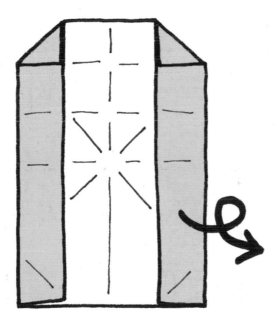

10. Turn over.

11. Make three valley folds, folding the top edge over and over and over . . .

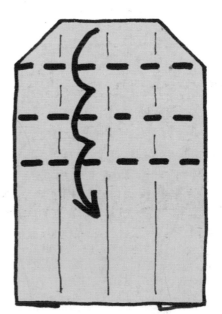

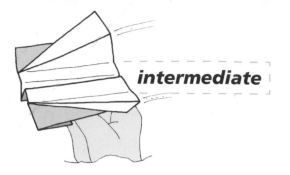

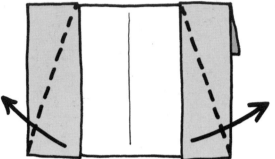

13. Fold the loose corners to the outside, as shown.

12. . . . like this. Turn over.

14. Fold the left edge across to the right, folding the model in half.

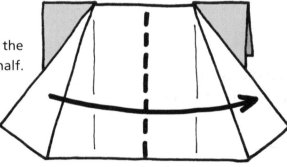

15. Fold down the front edge, folding dot to dot. Repeat behind.

16. To fly the Cutter, hold the model as shown. Hold it at the point of balance and launch it with a moderate throw. It should cleave its way speedily through the air, quicker than expected.

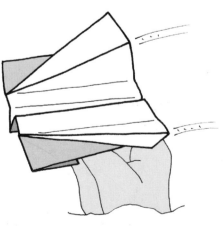

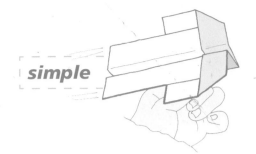

simple

T-GLIDER

The very first origami design I learned was taught to me by my father, when I was about 6 years old. It was a two-piece glider, in which a rectangle of paper was folded, and then the bottom edge was cut off and inserted as a tail. It was quite a complex design, but it made a great flyer, especially outdoors. My T-Glider uses a similar system of construction but is much simpler to make. It is a reliable flyer outdoors or indoors.

Begin with a sheet of regular 8½ x 11-inch copy paper or European A4 paper.

PREPARATION

1. Cut the paper in half.

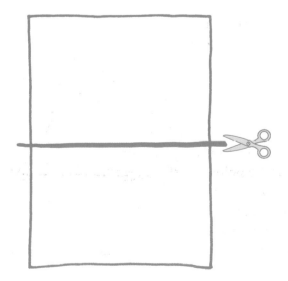

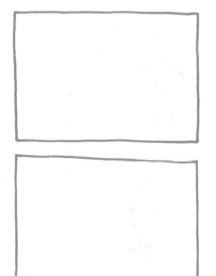

2. These are the two pieces. We will use them both.

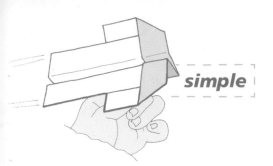

simple

NOSEPIECE

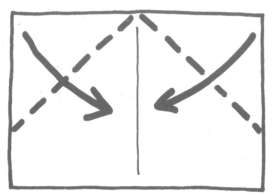

3. Fold and unfold one piece in half to find the center line, and then fold the top corners to the center line.

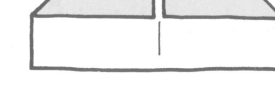

4. The nosepiece is complete.

TAIL PIECE

5. Fold and unfold the other piece in half to find the center line, and then fold the top corners to the center line.

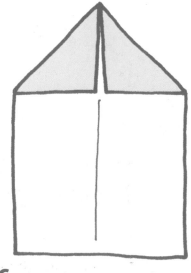

6. The tailpiece is complete.

ASSEMBLY

7. Insert the tailpiece into the nosepiece . . .

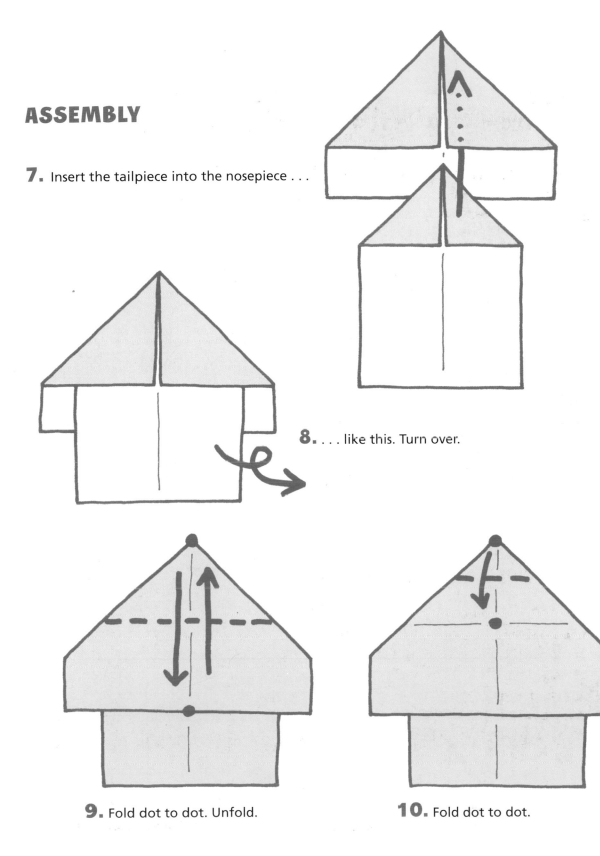

8. . . . like this. Turn over.

9. Fold dot to dot. Unfold.

10. Fold dot to dot.

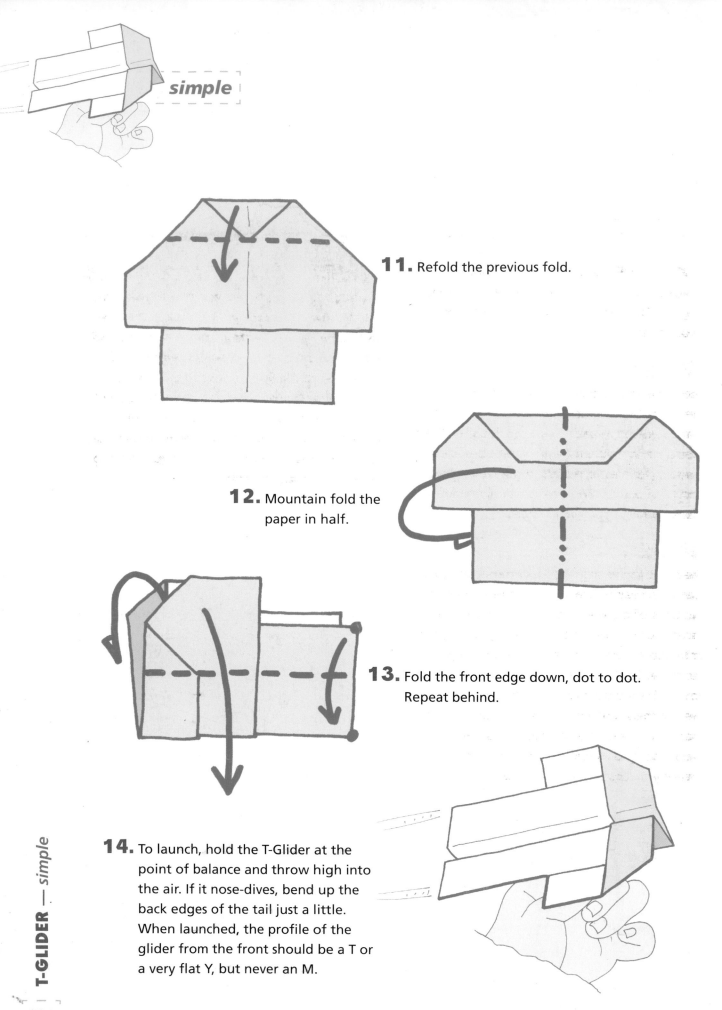

11. Refold the previous fold.

12. Mountain fold the paper in half.

13. Fold the front edge down, dot to dot. Repeat behind.

14. To launch, hold the T-Glider at the point of balance and throw high into the air. If it nose-dives, bend up the back edges of the tail just a little. When launched, the profile of the glider from the front should be a T or a very flat Y, but never an M.

RESOURCES

You've folded the models in this book and now, of course, you want to learn more about origami. Here are a few suggestions for more folding fun:

THE INTERNET

There are lots of excellent origami sites, and the list will doubtless continue to grow. Some feature a Web master's own work while others specialize in mathematical models, traditional models, geometric models, modular models, book reviews . . . and on and on. There are also many "how-to" origami movies.

BOOKS

There are hundreds of origami books in print in many languages. Buying from the Internet on the basis of a cover photo and perhaps a few spreads can be very hit-or-miss. If you can, find unbiased online reviews before making your purchase. Better yet, visit a good bookstore or library. The universal system of diagramming used in this book means that if you really want that Japanese or Russian book you saw, you should be able to understand the instructions, even if you don't read the language.

ORIGAMI ORGANIZATIONS

Frankly, you can only learn so much online or from books. It's when you meet other people interested in origami that you learn more and enjoy it more. There are organized origami societies and clubs in many cities. To find a group, simply run a Web search on "origami." In the United States, the premier origami organization is Origami USA: www.origami-usa .org. In Britain, it is the British Origami Society: www.britishorigami.info.

PAUL JACKSON *is a professional paper artist and instructor living in Tel Aviv. His work has been exhibited in museums and galleries around the world.*